WARNING!

Lots of crazy words!

© Matthew Hitch &
   Sunok Moon 2023

Author: Matthew Hitch

Co-author: Sunok Moon

Illustrator: Matthew Hitch

Cover Design: Brittany Hitch

Layout Design: Matthew Hitch

Text Design: Matthew Hitch

Image Manager: Matthew Hitch

~~Vain Meglomaniac: Matthew Hitch~~

Credits Editor: Matthew Hitch

Image Manager Manager: S. Moon

Image Manager Manager Control: Absolutely no one

Artistic Arguer: Sunok Moon

Dishwasher: Matthew Hitch
(occasionally Sunok Moon)

Title: Captain Matt's Super Crazy Fun

Preschool Phonics 4 Student Book

ISBN 979-711-982546-8-9

First published 2023

Published by Hitch Publishing

info@supercrazyfun.net

All rights reserved. No part of this publication may be reproduced, stored in a retrieval system, or transmitted, in any form or by any means, without the prior permission of the copyright holders, with the exception of small excerpts for review purposes or promotion of the contents or characters. This exception excludes any publication containing sexually explicit content, or content that may be perceived as "obscene."

This textbook came about as the result of 20 years of trying to make kids enjoy learning English. It is designed around the use of the rhotic R and other characteristics of English pronunciation common in North America. We believe it can be used in other parts of the world as most phonics books can, and we are keen to hear feedback from anyone who tries this.

We want to make clear that the word "crazy" used in the title is in relation to any of the common definitions illustrated below, and does not refer in any way to the meaning "insane."

strange/illogical   **wild**   **unexpected**   **fun**   **unwise**

About the Authors:

Matthew Hitch has taught English in Korea for the better part of 20 years and holds a master's degree in applied linguistics. He clearly does not have a pig nose, and by most accounts is not at all malodorous. He also cuts a dashing figure according to his wife.

Sunok Moon prefers to go by the name Michelle, and is in fact quite scary as reported in the bio on the back of this book. She has a degree in English literature and has taught English in Korea for approximately 3 weeks longer than Matthew, who is writing this and finds it weird to refer to himself in the third person.

Contents

Welcome parents and teachers!

Thank you for considering our book. Phonics books are notoriously boring, so this is the last bastion of publishing where even the tiniest bit of creativity can raise the bar (sorry phonics book publishers, but it's true). With that said, we humbly offer you our content. We have also intentionally challenged convention in a few ways. Much of what we have to say may be used or discarded though, and these books can be used just like any other mainstream phonics book. We hope you will choose to use whatever you please and dispose of the rest.

Please allow us to explain just where our method of teaching phonics may diverge from mainstream approaches, and please do forgive us for sharing information from what is undeniably the most mind-numbingly boring and seemingly useless field of study, linguistics. Most phonics books are not written by scholars in the field of linguistics. They are mostly written by early childhood educators, so perhaps that's the first divergence. We'll start with how we sound out consonants. In linguistic studies it is not uncommon for consonants to be distinguished by using a vowel (usually "ah") on both sides. This means a "V" sounds like "ahvah" and an "F" sounds like "ahfah" and so on. Most phonics books distinguish consonant sounds without such preceding vowel, but they do follow with a vowel in the form of the schwa. This is fine for most consonants, but the ones that are able to be maintained until breath is exhausted can be confusing with a schwa where they end a word. It's mostly ESL students who feel this confusion, but we think it doesn't hurt to teach those consonants without a schwa to native speakers as well, so where "V" sounds like "və" in most phonics books, in our book it is presented as "vvvvvvv" with no schwa. We apply this to all long consonant sounds in our audio files (L,M,N&R are also presented as long with a tiny schwa sound at the end though). If you have read this far, we take our hats off to you. Most would be fast asleep by now.

The next divergence is our use of Magic E. We chose Magic E for the fun potential. The Split Digraphs just can't seem to hold a crowd. Magic E is no longer used in most educational settings for many reasons, but mostly because as a rule it cannot be defined clearly. We do mention that split digraphs are better though, mainly to extend an olive branch to all the teachers we hope will buy our books.

And the final divergence we would like to mention is our choice of words. Our choice of words may seem a bit odd at times throughout the books, but we chose them for their potential for keeping kids engaged over their usefulness. We approach a phonics book as a tool to teach about sounds much more than vocabulary. Poop, vomit, spit, fart, snot, and burp are the most popular with our students. We tried to find a spot for booger, but alas...

Our word choice is also strange in that it includes words that have the long E vowel when teaching split digraphs. Most phonics books glance over the long E vowel. The argument we have heard for this is that it is difficult for the younger students, but we suspect that it's avoided more because it's difficult for authors to find suitable words. We decided to give it a try, and our experience is that the long E words we chose are not that difficult for our students to grasp. Given that English is their second language, we believe native English speaking kids will cope with them just fine. Also you may notice our sight words are not all actually sight words - oops! Anyway, we hope you enjoy our silly books.

Welcome students!

Now we will learn how to "blend" sounds!
Blend means "mix together."

But we don't actually put them in a blender!
It's more like we let them go down the waterslide together.

There is no room between blended sounds. They have to squeeze tightly together to make just one sound.

But that's just their sounds. We still leave a gap when we write them.

Let's get started...

Sounds

Vowels

There are two kinds of letters. The 5 letters below are called "vowels." The rest of the alphabet are called "consonants."

long sound (name) short sound

A   a 🙂

E   e 🙂

I   i 😐

O   o 😐

U   u 😐

Tracks 0-9

Track 5

i and u are very short!

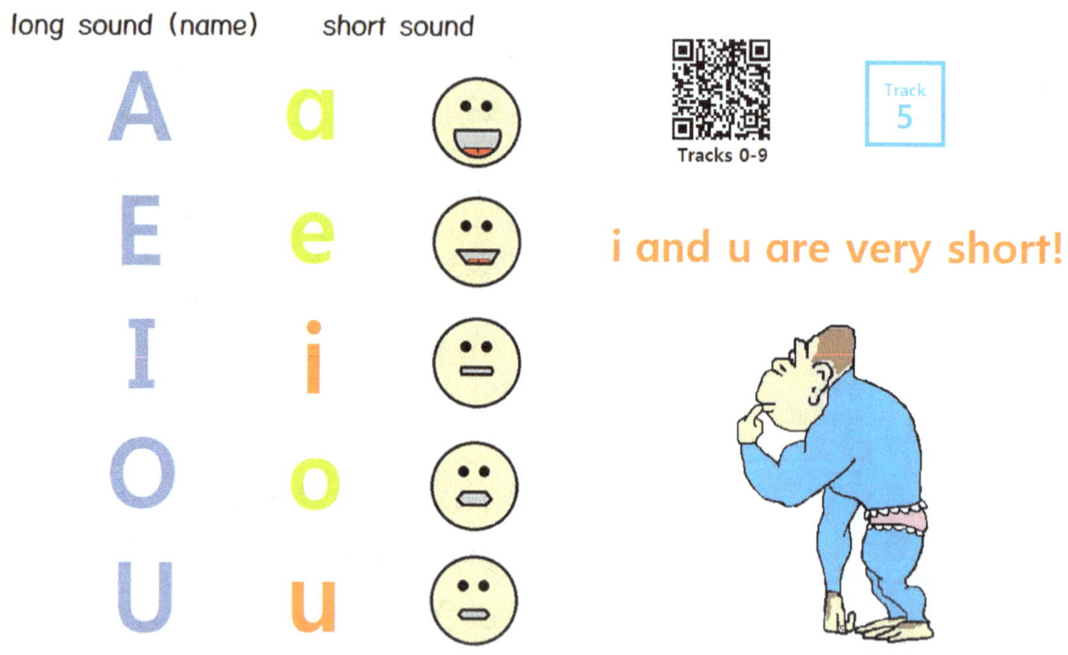

Some vowels can make a blend too, but let's talk about them in the next book!

Track 6

From here this book is just about consonants.

Sounds

Y is a spy!

Tracks 0-9

Y seems like a good consonant.

But Y really wants to be a vowel.

Y likes being an I.

Or even the long E sound!

So in a blend, Y prefers
to sound like a vowel.

Perhaps you can hear when
Y is being a vowel.

Double Consonants

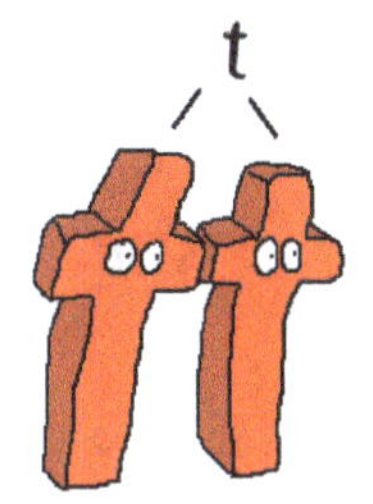

Double consonants are easy to understand. They just make
the same sound at the same time. And "ck" are like that too.

Listen, point, and make the sound:  Words with **bl br cl cr fl fr**

Tracks 0-9

Track 9

1   b + l = bl

2   c + r = cr

3   f + l = fl

Listen, point, and say the word:

Track 10

1   bl + ock = block

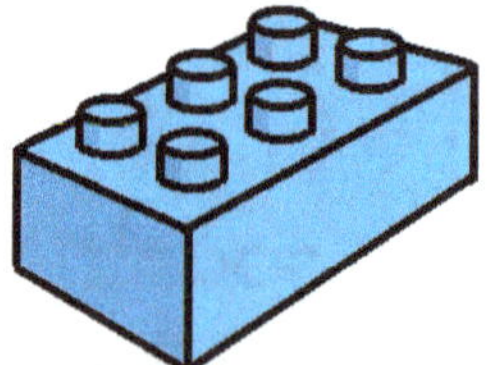

2   cr + ash = crash

3   fl + ag = flag

Follow the rules

1   br + ick = __________ 

2   cl + iff = __________ 

3   fr + ee = __________ 

4   cr + y = __________ 

New Words

Listen, point and repeat the new words

bl

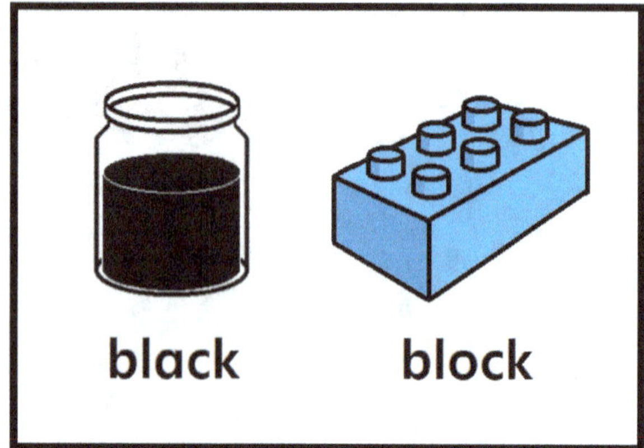

black   **block**

br

brag   **brick**

cl

cliff   **clock**

cr

crash   **cry**

fl

flag   **fly**

fr

free   **fry**

Exercises

Listen and complete the word

Tracks 10-19

1  ___ y

2  ___ y

3  ___ ock

4  ___ ack

Listen and circle the right letters AND picture

1 bl cl fl  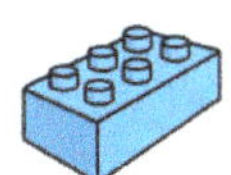 

2 bl cr fl   

3 br cl fl   

4 br cr fr   

5 bl cr fr   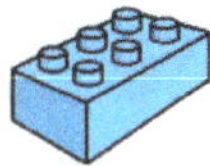

6 br cl fr   

Exercises

Circle the word you hear

Track 14

Tracks 10-19

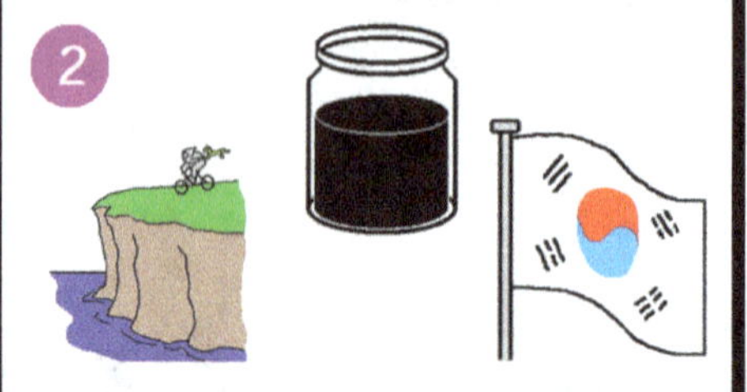

Circle the sound you hear

Track 15

1. cl fr br   2. bl fl cr

3. fl br cr   4. cl bl fr

Chant

Track 16

Fly the flag
Fly the flag
Fly the black flag!

Crash into a cliff

Fry the flag
Fry the flag
Fry the black flag!

Story

Write the word to match the picture

1 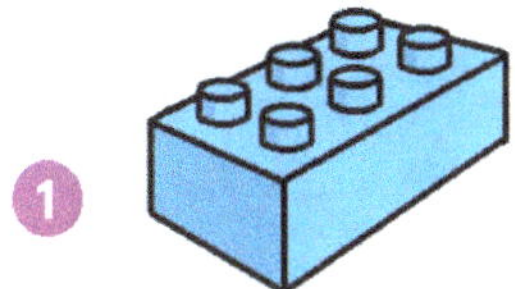

2 

3 

4 

Listen and read along

New sight words: look   can   be

UNIT 2   Consonant Blends

Listen, point, and make the sound:    Words with **gl gr pl pr sl dr**

Tracks 10-19

Track 18

1   g + l = gl

2   d + r = dr

3   p + l = pl

Listen, point, and say the word: **Track 19**

1   gl + ove = glove

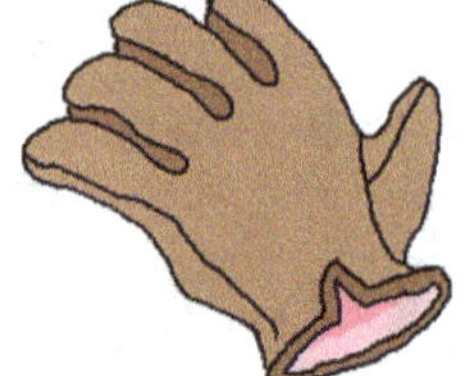

2   dr + ive = drive

3   pl + um = plum

Follow the rules

Write the words

1 sl + ed = __________ 

2 gr + een = __________ 

3 pr + ess = __________ 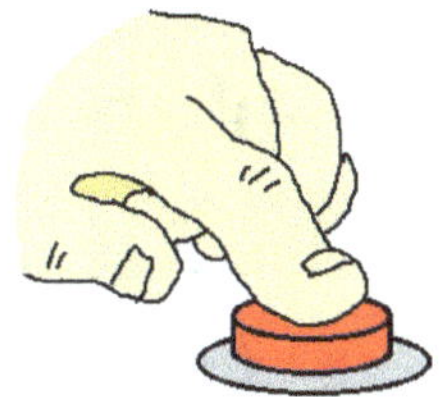

4 dr + ess = __________ 

New Words

Listen, point and repeat the new words

Track 20

gl

glass glove

gr

grape green

pl

plan plum

pr

press price

dr

dress drive

sl

sled slug

Exercises

Listen and complete the word

1  _______ ug   2  _______ ass

3  _______ ice   4 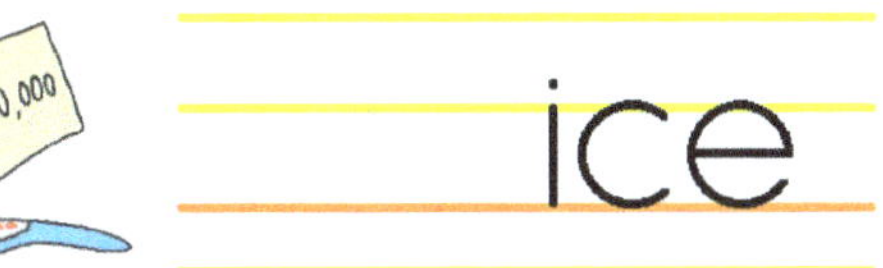 _______ an

Listen and circle the right letters AND picture

1 pl gr sl 

2 gl pl sl 

3 dr gr gl 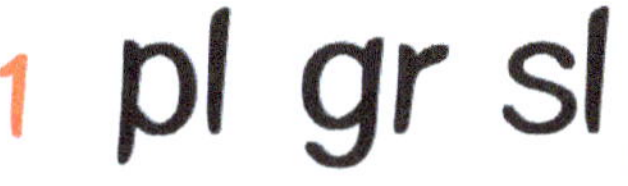

4 gr pr dr 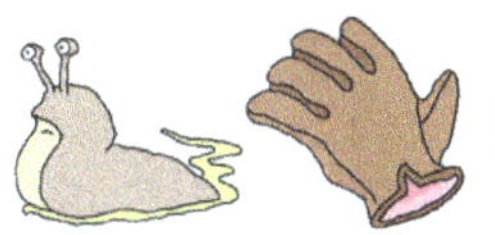

5 sl pr dr 

6 pl pr gl 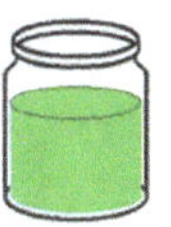

Exercises

Circle the word you hear

Tracks 20-29

Track 23

Circle the sound you hear

Track 24

1 dr gl pl   2 sl gr pr

3 pr pl gr   4 dr gl sl

Chant

Track 25

New sight words: onto

Green dress and gloves!

Green dress and gloves!

Press your face onto the glass

Green dress and gloves!

Story

Write the word to match the picture

 1

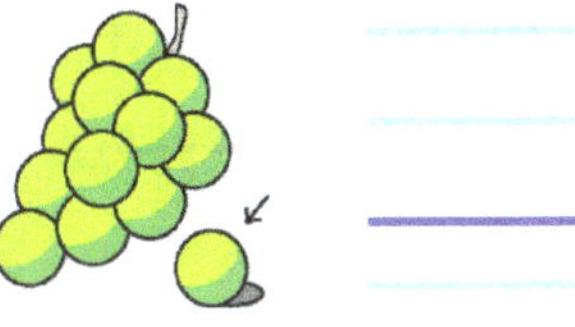 3

 2

 3

 4

Listen and read along

New sight words: are too we ready

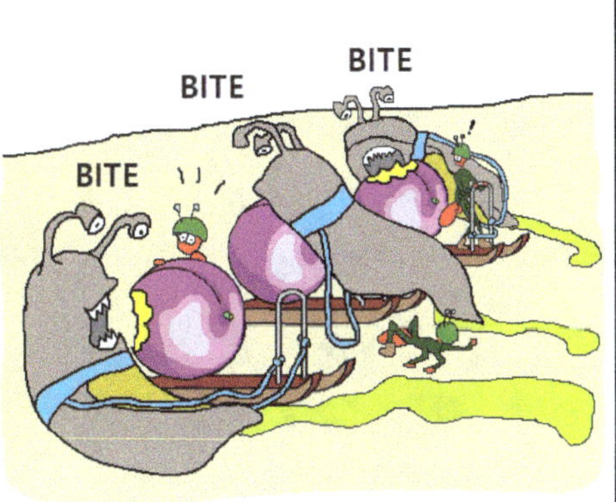

More Sounds

The Story of Q and U

Tracks 20-29

Q and U are married! They are very different. Everyone at the wedding thought a vowel and a consonant were too different to get married, but they didn't care!

U is very outgoing. He often goes out without Q, but Q almost never goes anywhere without U.

Q is almost always with U. When they are together, U is silent. They are very happy together.

More Sounds

Blends are everywhere!

Some blends can start words and some can end them, and some can do both!

And some just sit in the middle!

Tracks 20-29

G is a prankster

When N and G are together,
G pinches N's nose!
N can't make its usual sound.

So N covers G's mouth so it can't say anything at all!

Just sometimes if they are together in the middle of a word G can make a sound, though.

Listen and practice the "ng" sound:

1 ang   2 eng   3 ing   4 ong   5 ung

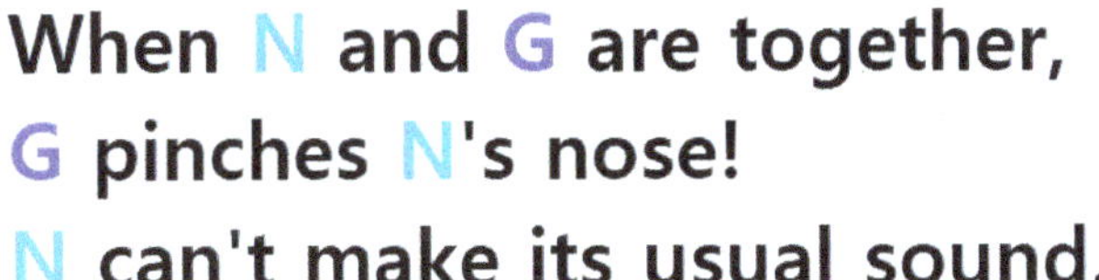

Listen, point, and make the sound:  Words with -ld -lt -nd -ng -nk -nt

Tracks 30-39

Track 31

1 n + t = nt

2 n + k = nk

3 n + g = ng

Listen, point, and say the word: Track 32

1 hu + nt = hunt

2 ta + nk = tank

3 ki + ng = king

Follow the rules 

Write the words

1 ha + nd = __________ 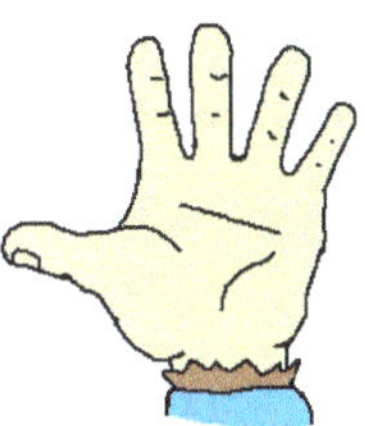

2 qui + lt = __________ 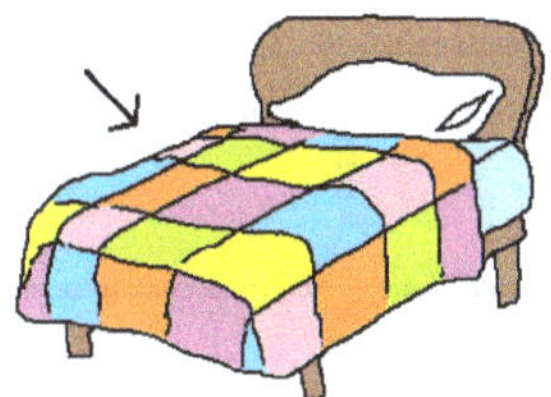

3 co + ld = __________ 

4 lo + ng = __________ 

New Words

Listen, point and repeat the new words

Track 33

-ld

cold   wild

-lt

melt   quilt

-nd

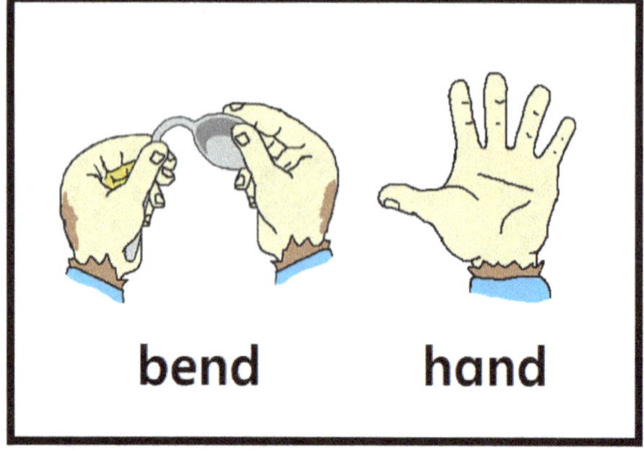

bend   hand

-ng

king   long

-nk

tank   think

-nt

hunt   plant

Exercises

Listen and complete the word

1  hu______

2  wi______

3  pla______

4  ki______

Listen and circle the right letters AND picture

1 -nt -nk -nd   

2 -ld -nk -ng   

3 -nt -lt -ng 

4 -nd -nk -ld  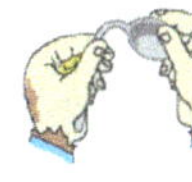 

5 -nd -lt -nt 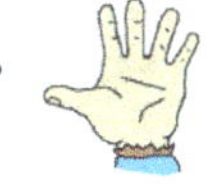 

6 -ng -ld -lt   

Exercises

Circle the word you hear

Track 36

Tracks 30-39

 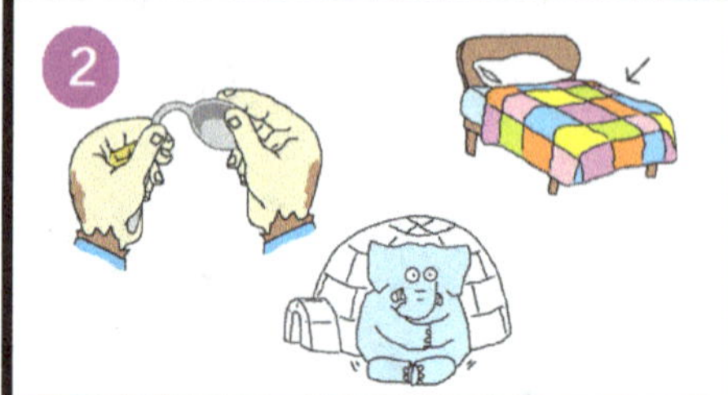 

Circle the sound you hear

Track 37

1. -ng   -ld   -nt   2. -nk   -nd   -lt

3. -nd   -ng   -lt   4. -nt   -ld   -nk

Chant

Track 38

Hunt hunt the wild wild plant

Put it in the zoo

A tank for the hunt

A quilt for the cold

A hat and gloves too

Story

Write the word to match the picture

1. _______________

2. _______________

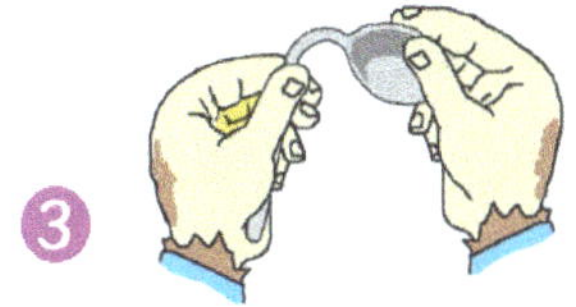
3. _______________

4. _______________

Listen and read along

Tracks 30-39

New sight words: again

Review

1

| 1 black | 2 block | 3 brag | 4 brick | 5 cliff | 6 clock |
| 7 crash | 8 cry | 9 flag | 10 fly | 11 free | 12 fry |

2

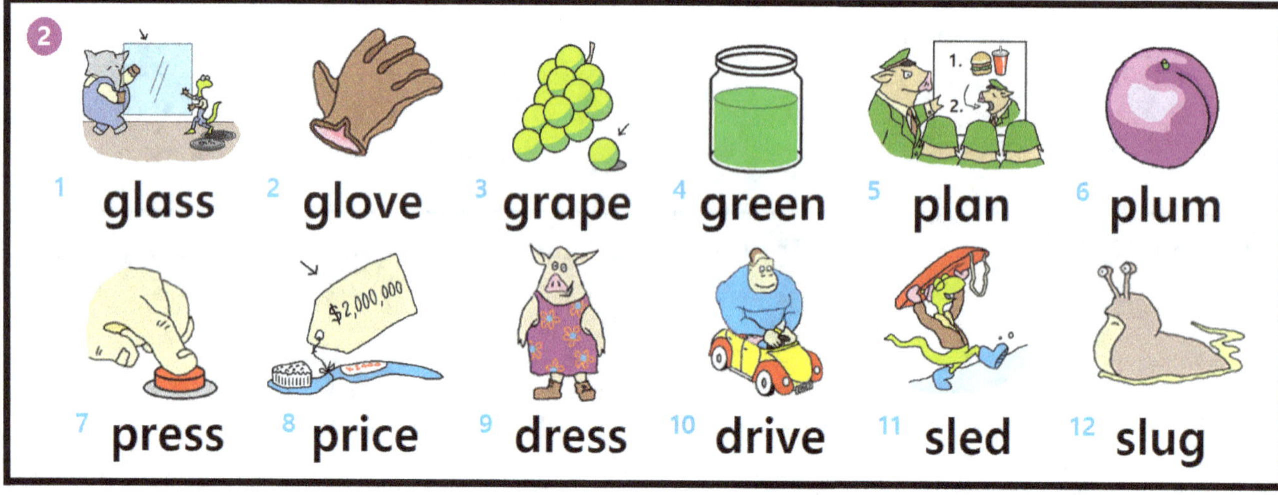

| 1 glass | 2 glove | 3 grape | 4 green | 5 plan | 6 plum |
| 7 press | 8 price | 9 dress | 10 drive | 11 sled | 12 slug |

3

| 1 cold | 2 wild | 3 melt | 4 quilt | 5 bend | 6 hand |
| 7 king | 8 long | 9 tank | 10 think | 11 hunt | 12 plant |

Review

1  ___y

2  ki___

3 ___ape

4 ___ock

5 ta___

6 ___ice

7 ___ag

8 ha___

Find the path

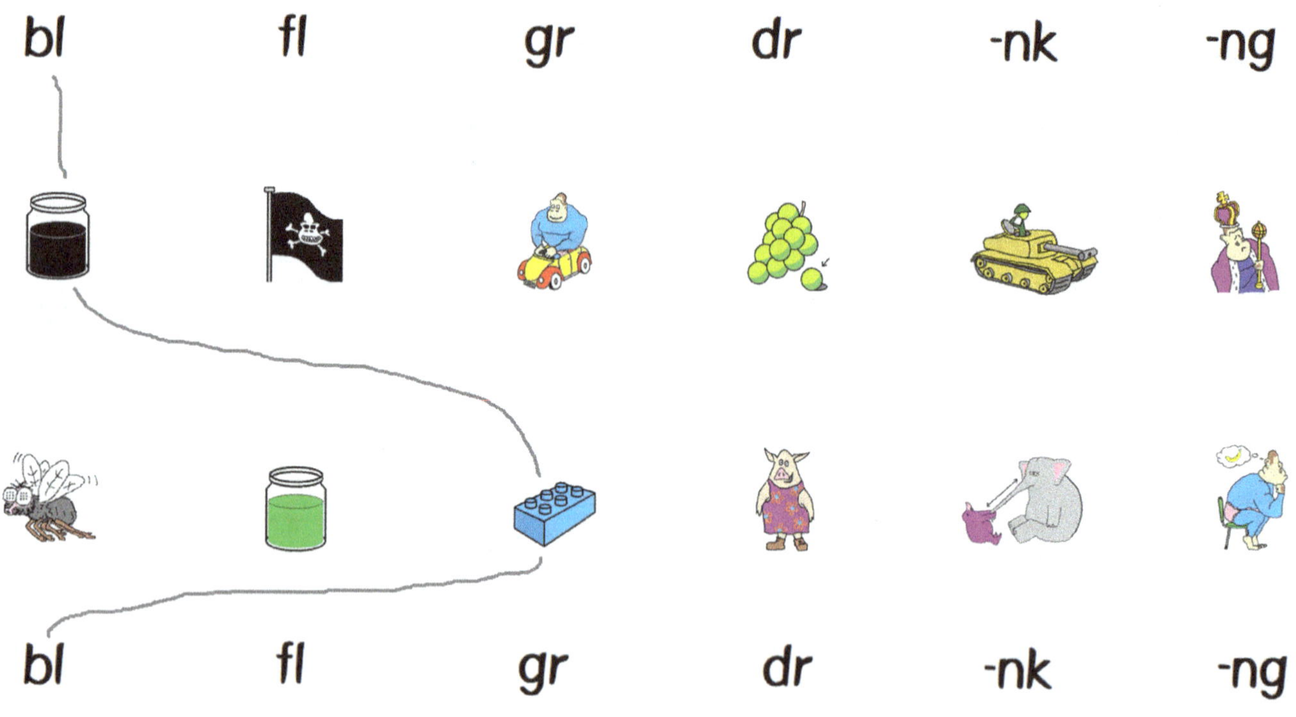

bl   fl   gr   dr   -nk   -ng

bl   fl   gr   dr   -nk   -ng

Listen and circle the right word

Tracks 40-49

Track 41

1 

2

3

4

Review

Listen and circle. Then write the number in the word list.

1

2

3

4

5

6

wild	☐	plum	☐
green	☐	think	☐
free	☐	glass	☐

UNIT 4   Consonant Blends

Listen, point, and make the sound: 

Tracks 40-49

Words with ph ch sh -ph -ch -sh

Track 43

1   p + h = ph

2   c + h = ch

3   s + h = sh

Listen, point, and say the word: **Track 44**

1   ph + one = phone 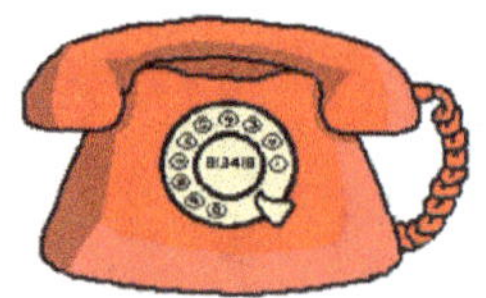

2   ri + ch = rich 

3   sh + ip = ship 

Follow the rules

1 gra + ph = __________

2 ch + in = __________

3 pu + sh = __________

4 ph + oto = __________

New Words

Tracks 40-49

Listen, point and repeat the new words

Track 45

ch

chin   chop

-ch

much   rich

ph

phone   photo

-ph

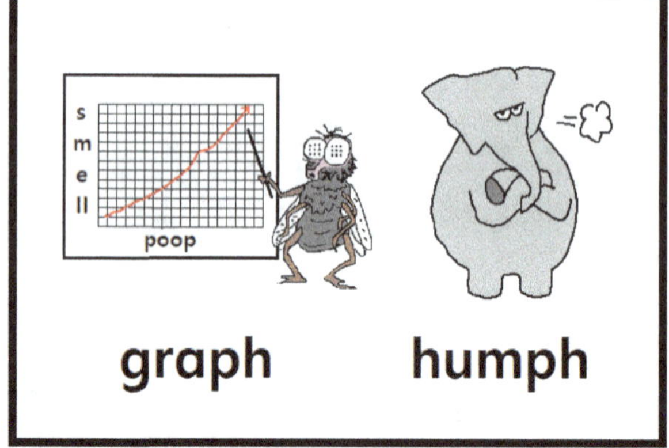

graph   humph

sh

shake   ship

-sh

cash   push

Exercises

Listen and complete the word

1  __ake   2 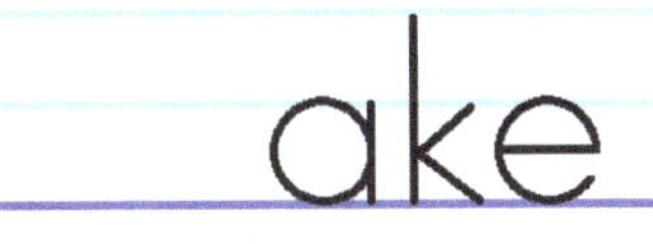 ca__

3  mu__   4  __hum

Listen and circle the right letters AND picture

1 sh -ch ph    2 sh -ch ph 

3 -sh ch -ph    4 -sh ch -ph  

5 -sh ch -ph     6 sh -ch ph   

Exercises

Circle the word you hear

Tracks 40-49

Circle the sound you hear

1 sh ch ph   2 sh ch ph

3 sh ch ph   4 sh ch ph

Chant

New sight words: his   how   check

Rich man on his ship
How much? How much?
Check the graph!

Rich man on the phone
How much? How much?
Check the cash!

Story

Write the word to match the picture

Listen and read along

New sight words: wow take

Listen, point, and make the sound:  Words with th sp sm -th -sp tr

Tracks 50-59

Track 52

1   t + h = th

2   s + p = sp

3   t + r = tr

Listen, point, and say the word:

Track 53

1 th + ick = thick 

2 wa + sp = wasp 

3 tr + uck = truck

Follow the rules 

Write the words

1 ba + th = _______________ 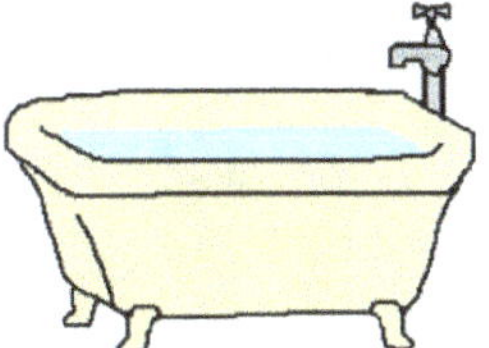

2 sp + it = _______________

3 sm + oke = _______________ 

4 th + in = _______________ 

New Words

Tracks 50-59

Listen, point and repeat the new words

Track 54

th

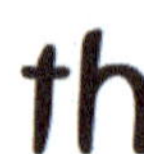

thick   thin

-th

bath   moth

sp

space   spit

-sp

gasp   wasp

sm

smile   smoke

tr

trash   truck

Exercises

Listen and complete the word

Track 55

Tracks 50-59

1   ick

2 oke

3   ash

4 ga

Listen and circle the right letters AND picture

Track 56

1 sp sm th   

2 sp tr th   

3 -sp sm -th  

4 -sp tr -th  

5 -sp sm -th   

6 sp tr th   

Exercises

Circle the word you hear

Track 57

Tracks 50-59

Circle the sound you hear

Track 58

1. sp sm th

2. sp tr th

3. sp tr th

4. sp sm th

Chant

Track 59

New sight words: choke

Trash truck in the thick black smoke

Choke and spit and gasp

Trash truck in the thick black smoke

I think I need a bath

Story

Write the word to match the picture

 1

 2

 3

 4

Listen and read along

Listen, point, and make the sound:  Words with st sk sc sn -st -sk -sc sw

Tracks 60-69

 Track 61

1   s + t = st

2   s + k = sk

3   s + n = sn

Listen, point, and say the word: Track 62

1   st + op = stop 

2   ma + sk = mask 

3   sn + ake = snake 

Follow the rules 

Write the words

1 ve + st = ________ 

2 sc + uba = ________ 

3 sw + im = ________ 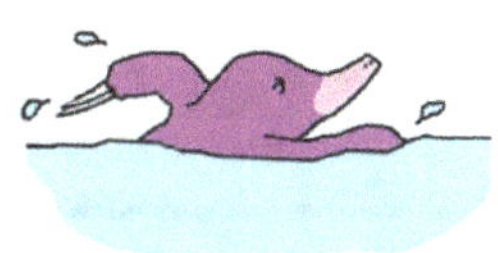

4 sn + ore = ________ 

New Words

Listen, point and repeat the new words

Track 63

st

stop   strong

-st

fast   vest

sc / sk

scuba   sky

-sc / -sk

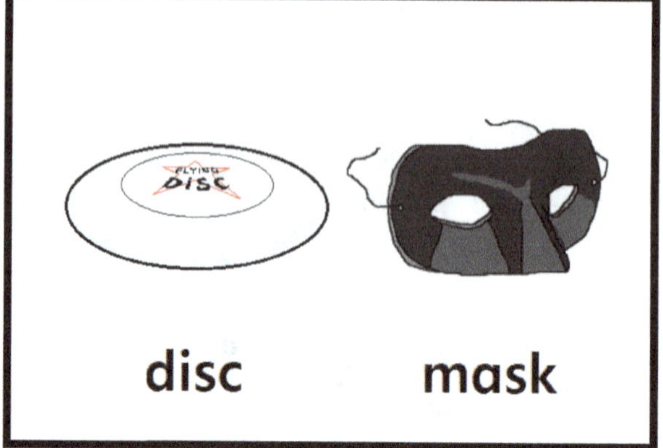

disc   mask

sn

snake   snore

sw

swan   swim

Exercises

Listen and complete the word

Tracks 60-69

1  _____ an   2  _____ rong

3  fa _____   4  ma _____

Listen and circle the right letters AND picture

1 st sn sk 

2 st sw sc 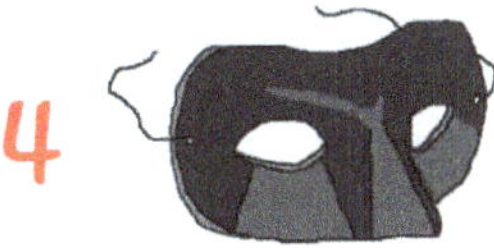

3 -st sn -sk 

4 -st sw -sk 

5 -st sn -sc 

6 st sw sc 

Exercises

Circle the word you hear

Circle the sound you hear

1.   st   sn   sk   2.   st   sw   sk

3.   st   sw   sc   4.   st   sn   sc

Chant

New sight words: as

Snake in a scuba mask
Swimming in the sea
Strong and fast
As he can be

Swan in a scuba mask
Swimming in the sea
Strong and fast
As he can be

Story

Write the word to match the picture

1.

2.

3.

4.

Listen and read along

Track 69

Tracks 60-69

New sight words: here sleep

Track 70

Tracks 70-79

Review

Listen, point, and repeat all the words

Tracks 70-79

Review

1 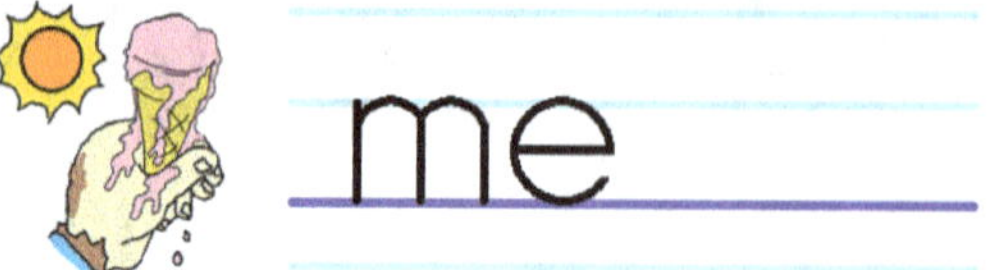 me

2  it

3  ash

4  one

5  fa

6  an

7  mo

8  op

Review

Listen and circle. Then write the number in the word list.

Tracks 70-79

1 

2  

3  

4  

5  

6  

bath ☐ plant ☐

melt ☐ vest ☐

ship ☐ photo ☐

Test

Listen and circle

Tracks 70-79

a  b  c 

1      

2    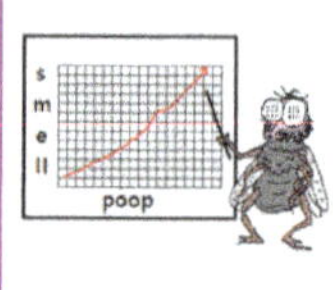  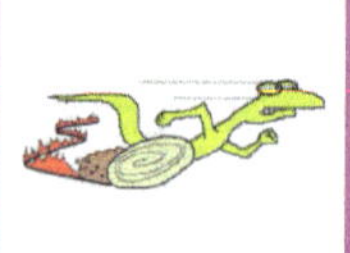

3   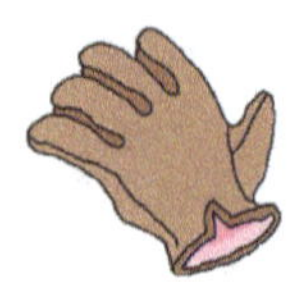   

4     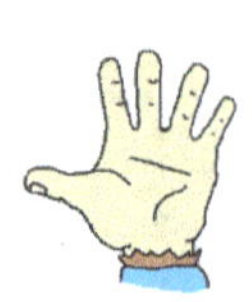 

5      

Test

Listen and write the blend (or digraph)

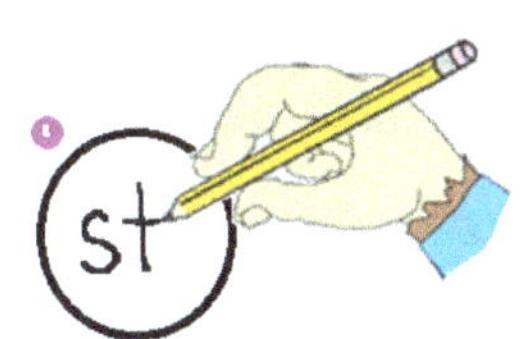

Tracks 70-79

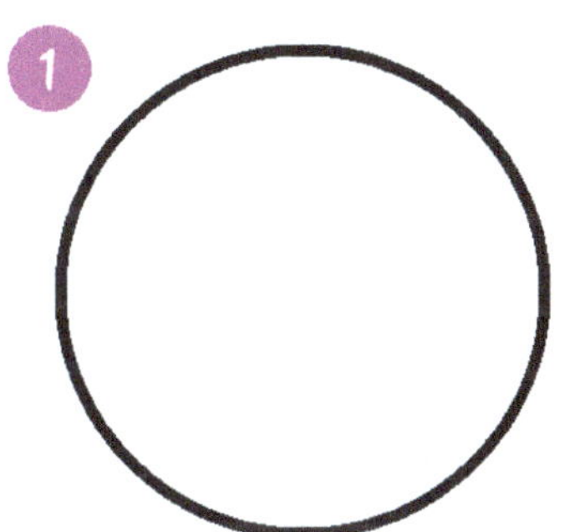

1

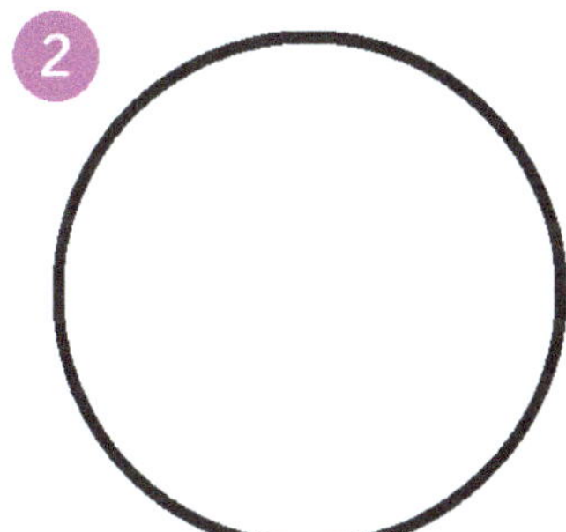

2

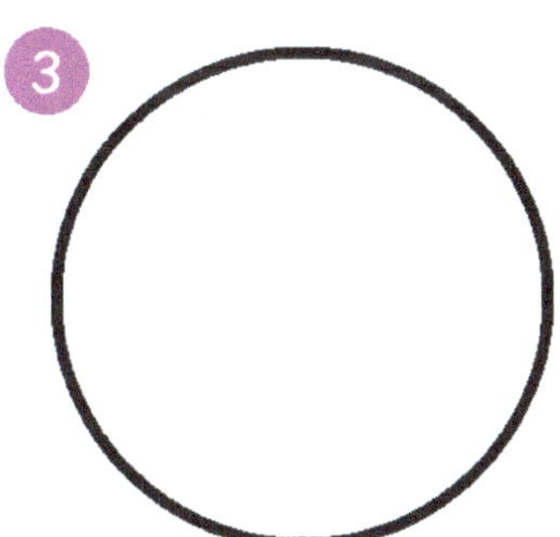

3

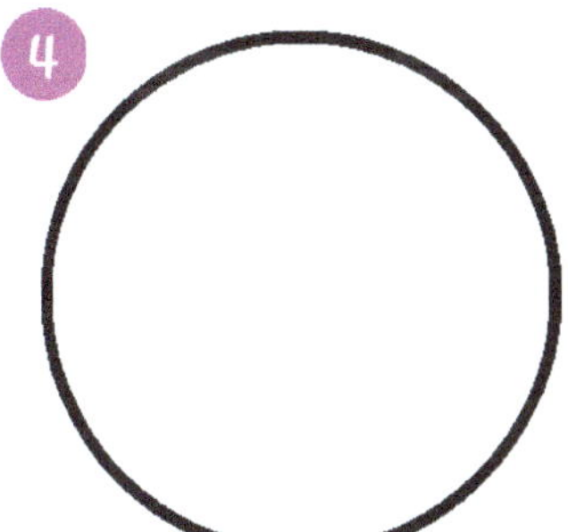

4

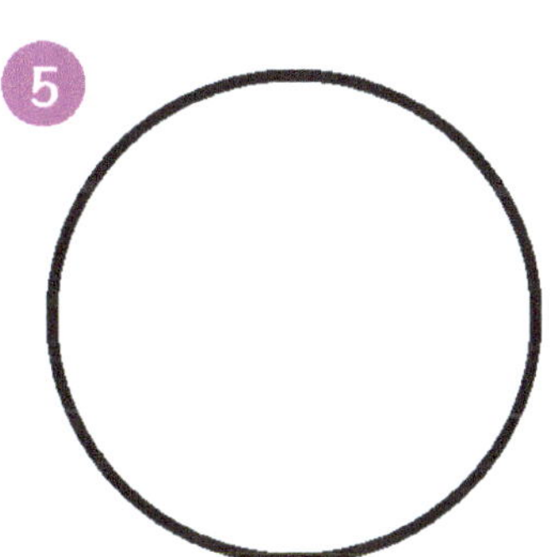

5

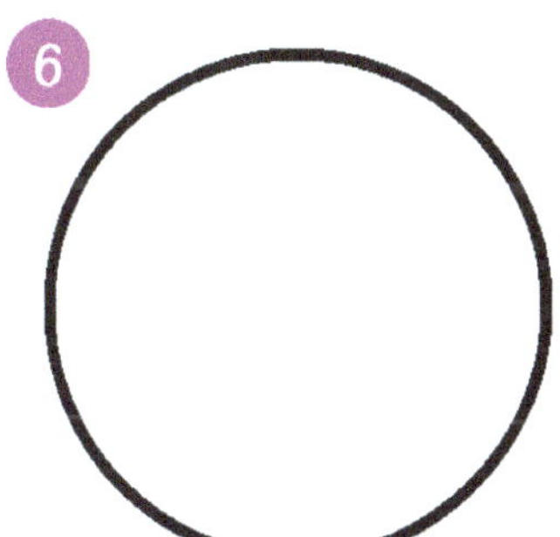

6

Test 

Listen and circle

Tracks 70-79

a **Track 79** b **Track 80** c **Track 81**

1		sm	dr	th	sw	-sk

2		tr	-nk	-sp	ph	cr

3		-ng	sc	ch	-st	-lt

4		fr	pr	sp	st	-nt

5		bl	gr	sh	sl	fl

Choose a picture and write the word to match

1 

2 

3 

4 

This is the end
of the book!

Word List

Unit 1

 black	block	brag	brick
 cliff	clock	crash	cry
flag	fly	free	fry

Unit 2

glass	glove	grape	green
plan	plum	press	price
dress	drive	sled	slug

Unit 3

cold	wild	melt	quilt
bend	hand	king	long
tank	think	hunt	plant

Word List

Unit 4

chin

chop

much

rich

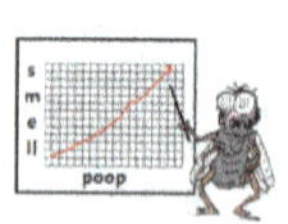
phone

photo

graph

humph

shake

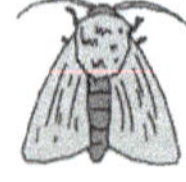
ship

cash

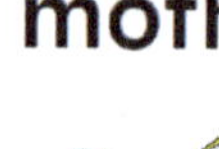
push

Unit 5

thick

thin

bath

moth

space

spit

gasp

wasp

smile

smoke

trash

truck

Unit 6

stop

strong

fast

vest

scuba

sky

disc

mask

snake

snore

swan

swim

OUR SIGHT WORD FLASH CARDS!

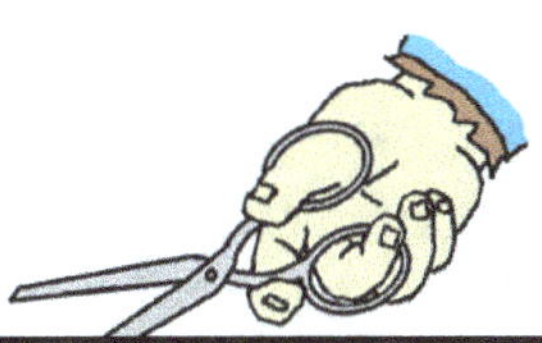

look

can

be

onto

are

too

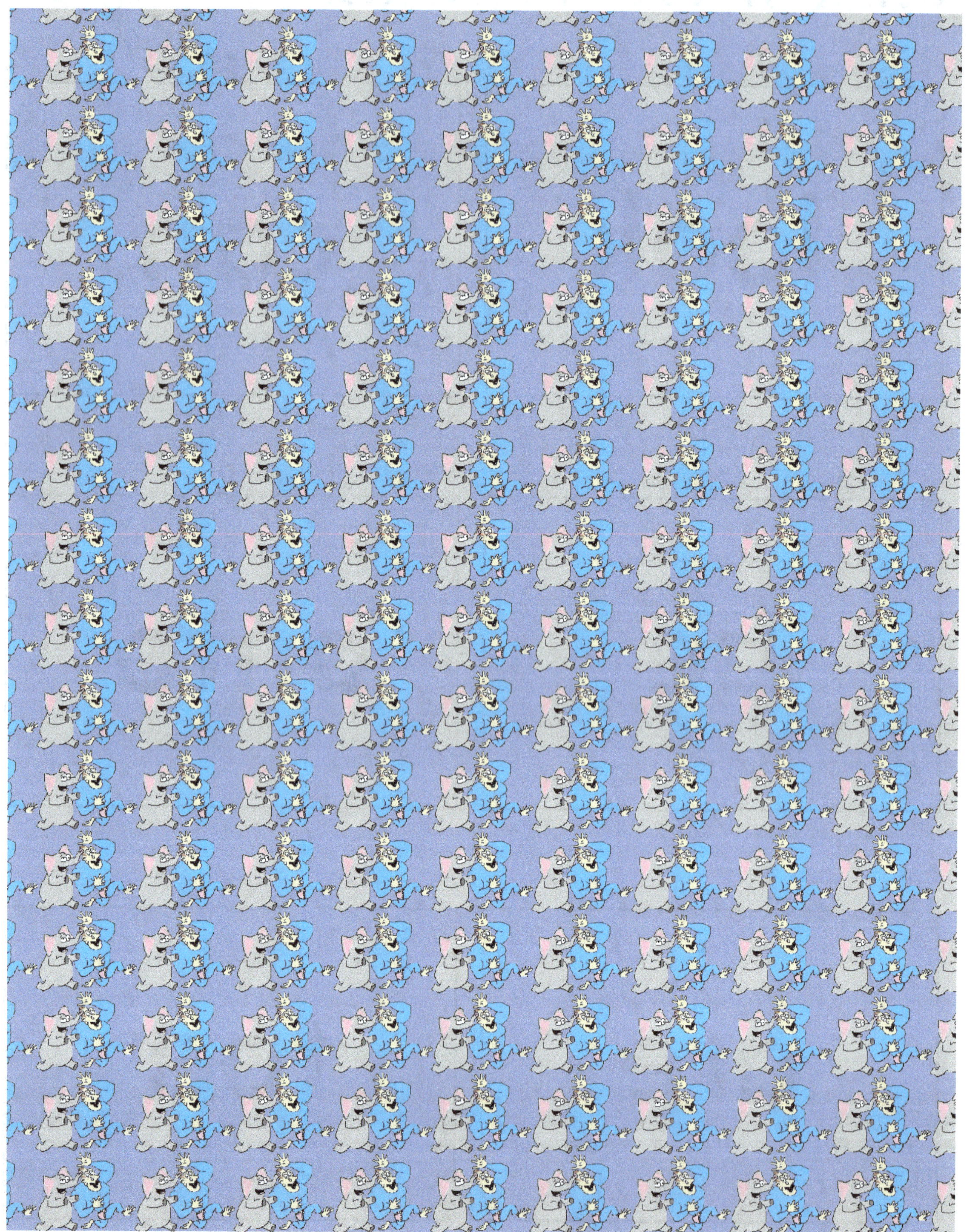

OUR SIGHT WORD FLASH CARDS!

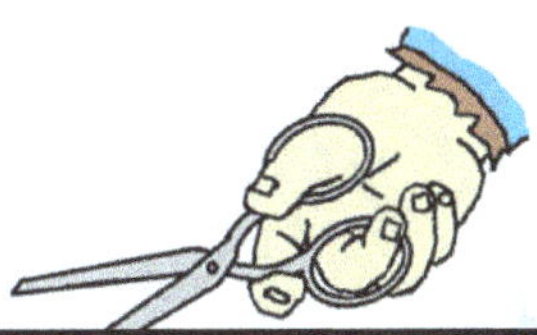

we

ready

again

his

how

check

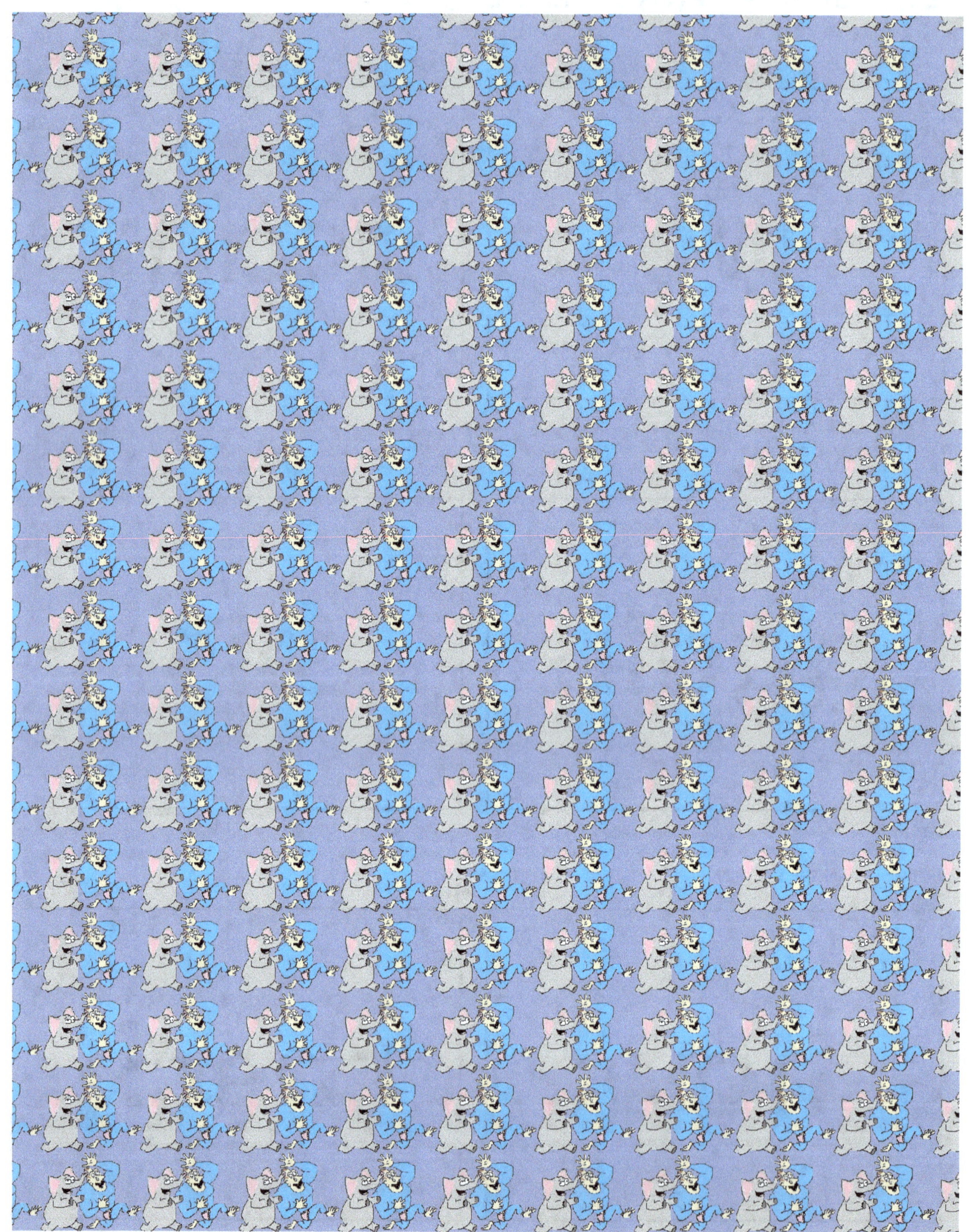

OUR SIGHT WORD FLASH CARDS!

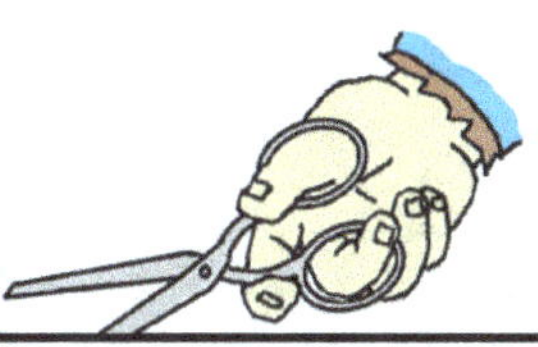

wow

take

choke

as

here

sleep

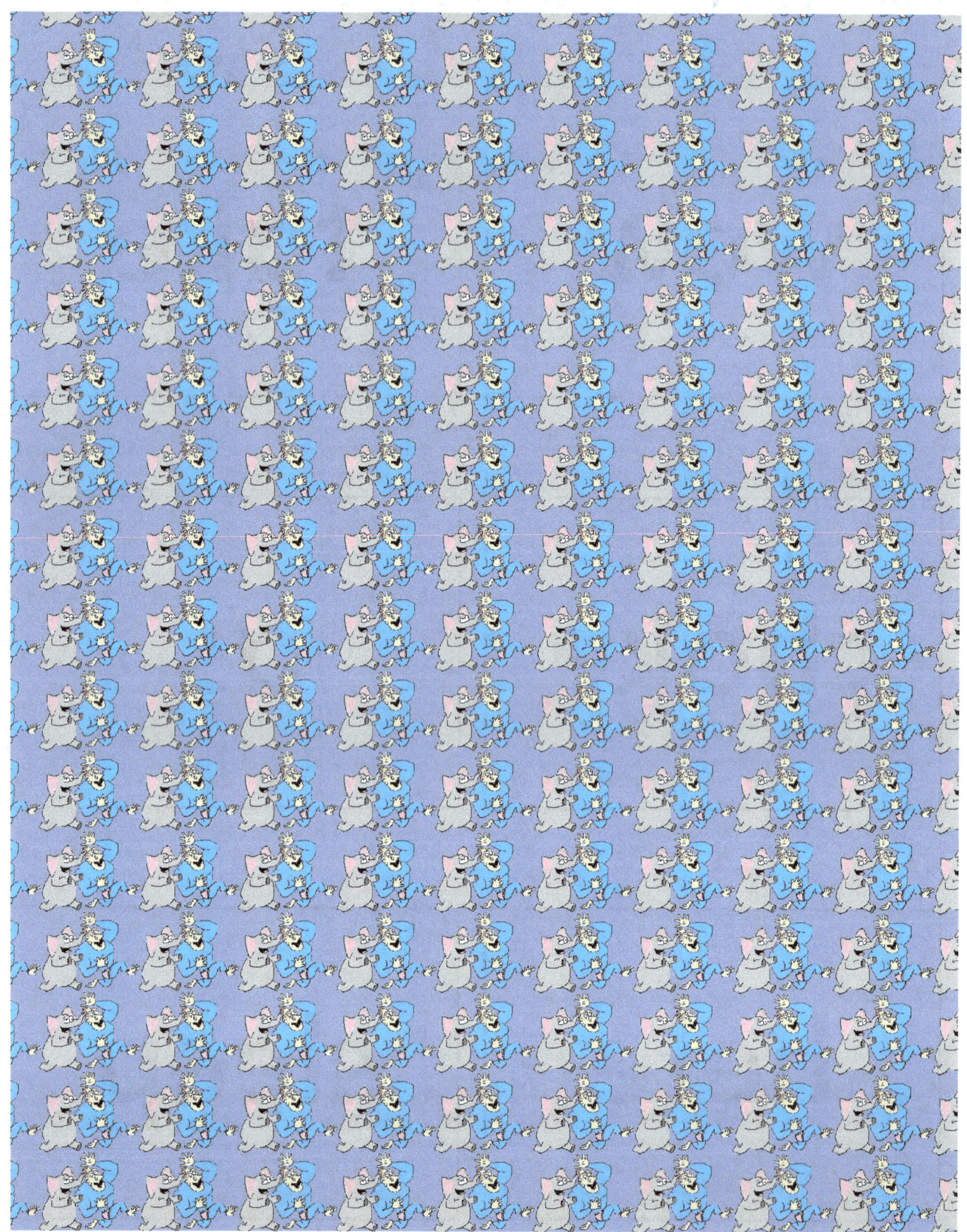

OUR SIGHT WORD FLASH CARDS!

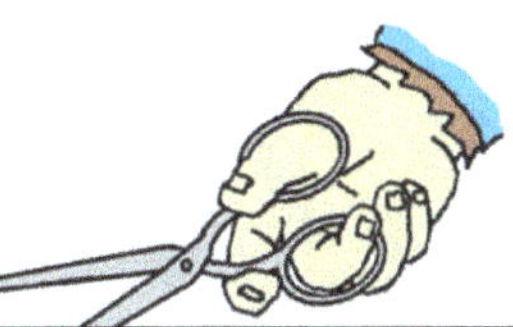

don't

play

at

but

after

for

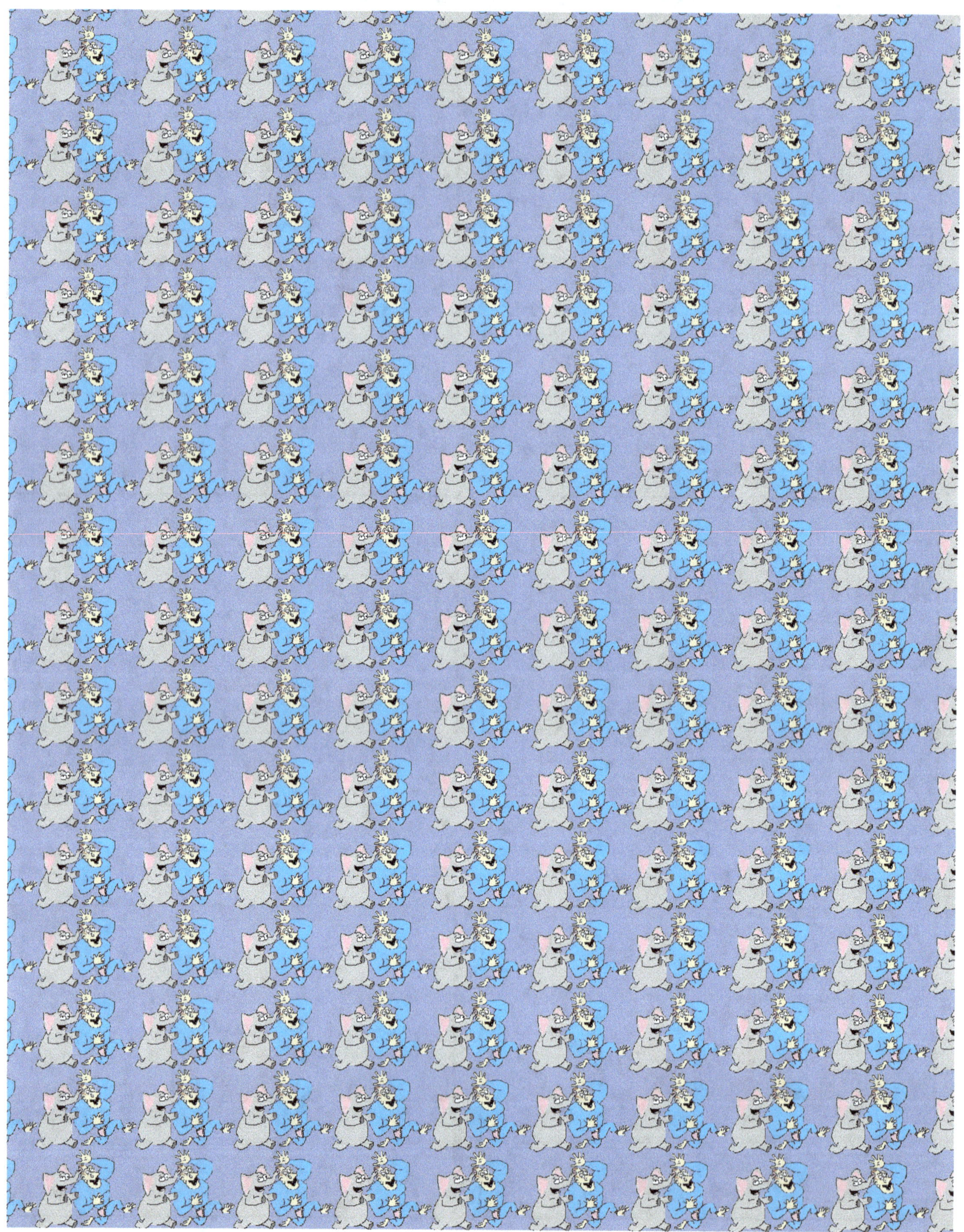

OUR SIGHT WORD FLASH CARDS!

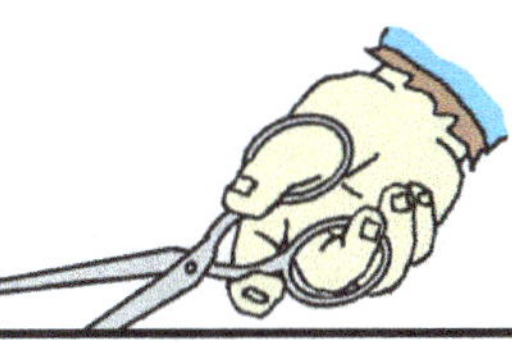

best

make

him

people

yell

my

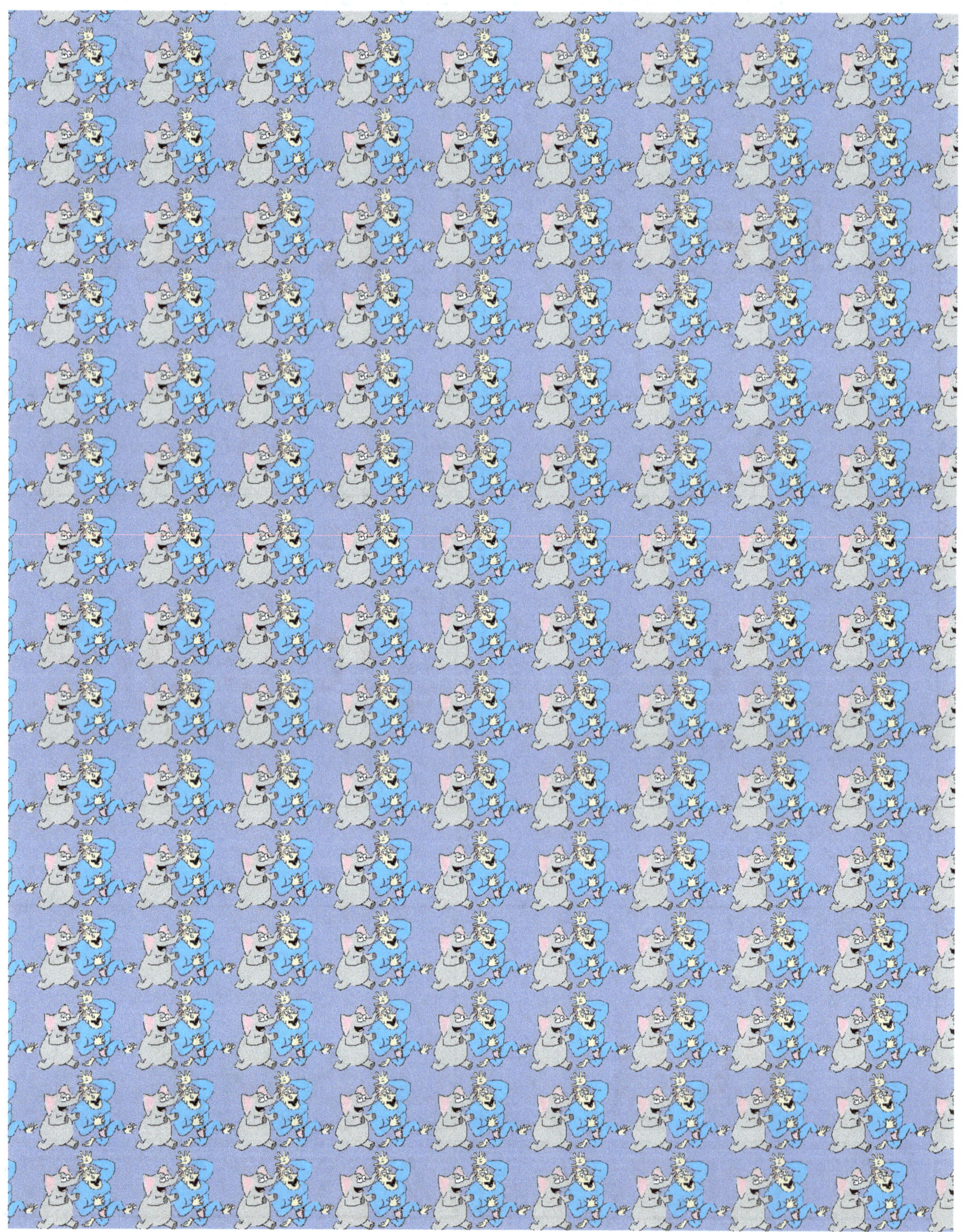

OUR SIGHT WORD FLASH CARDS!

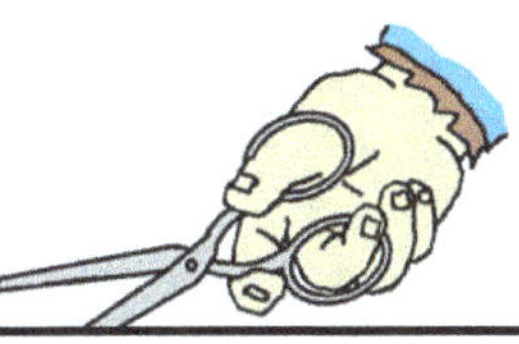

am

she

wear

so

will

want

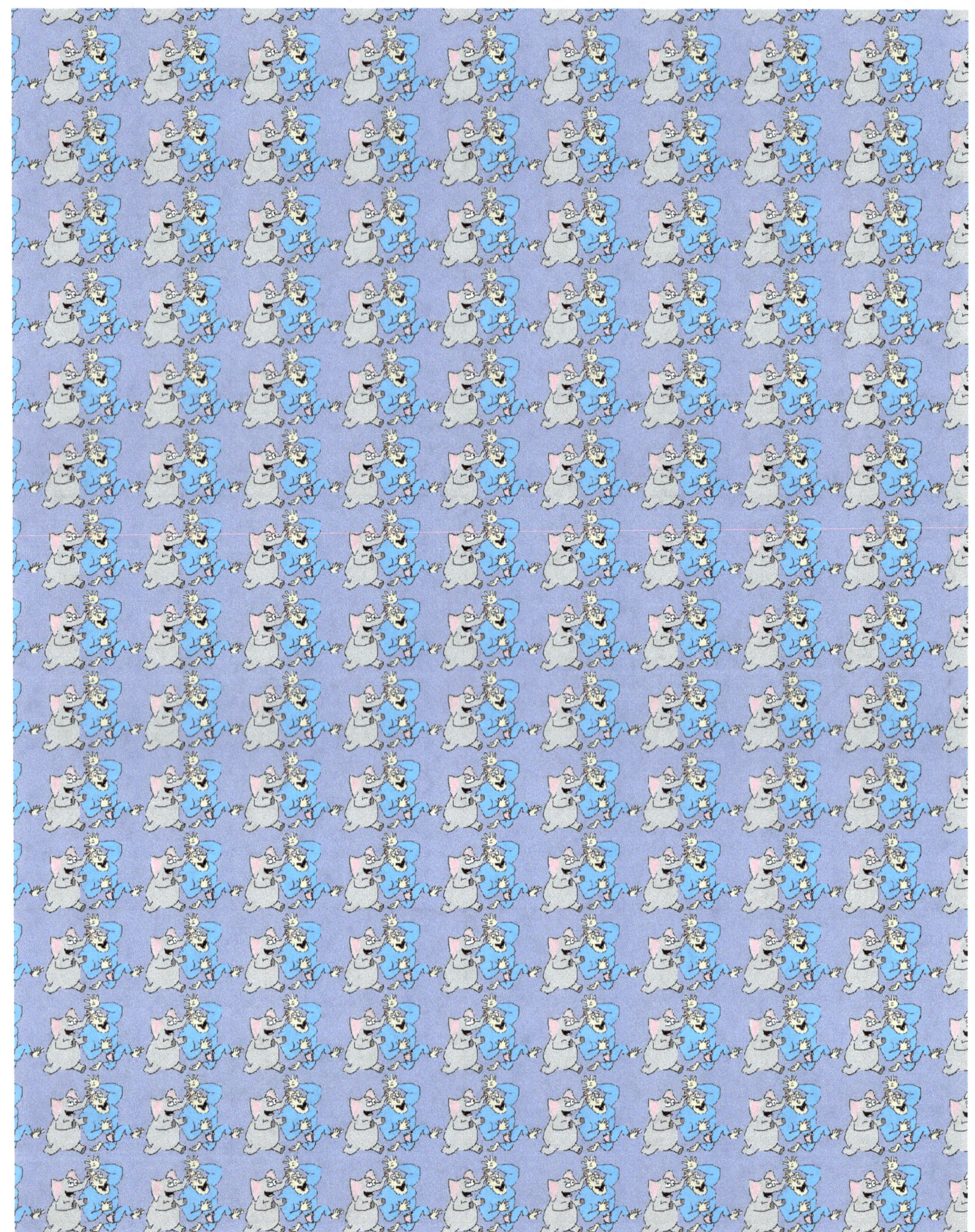

OUR SIGHT WORD FLASH CARDS!

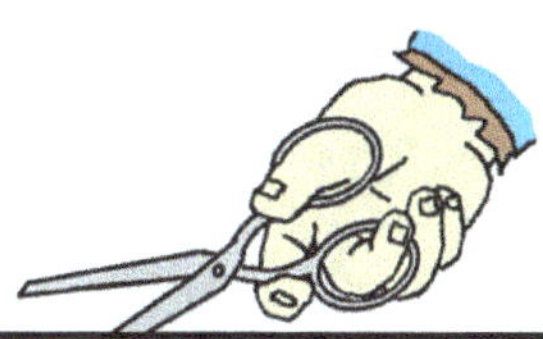

give

me

have

he

handsome

pretty

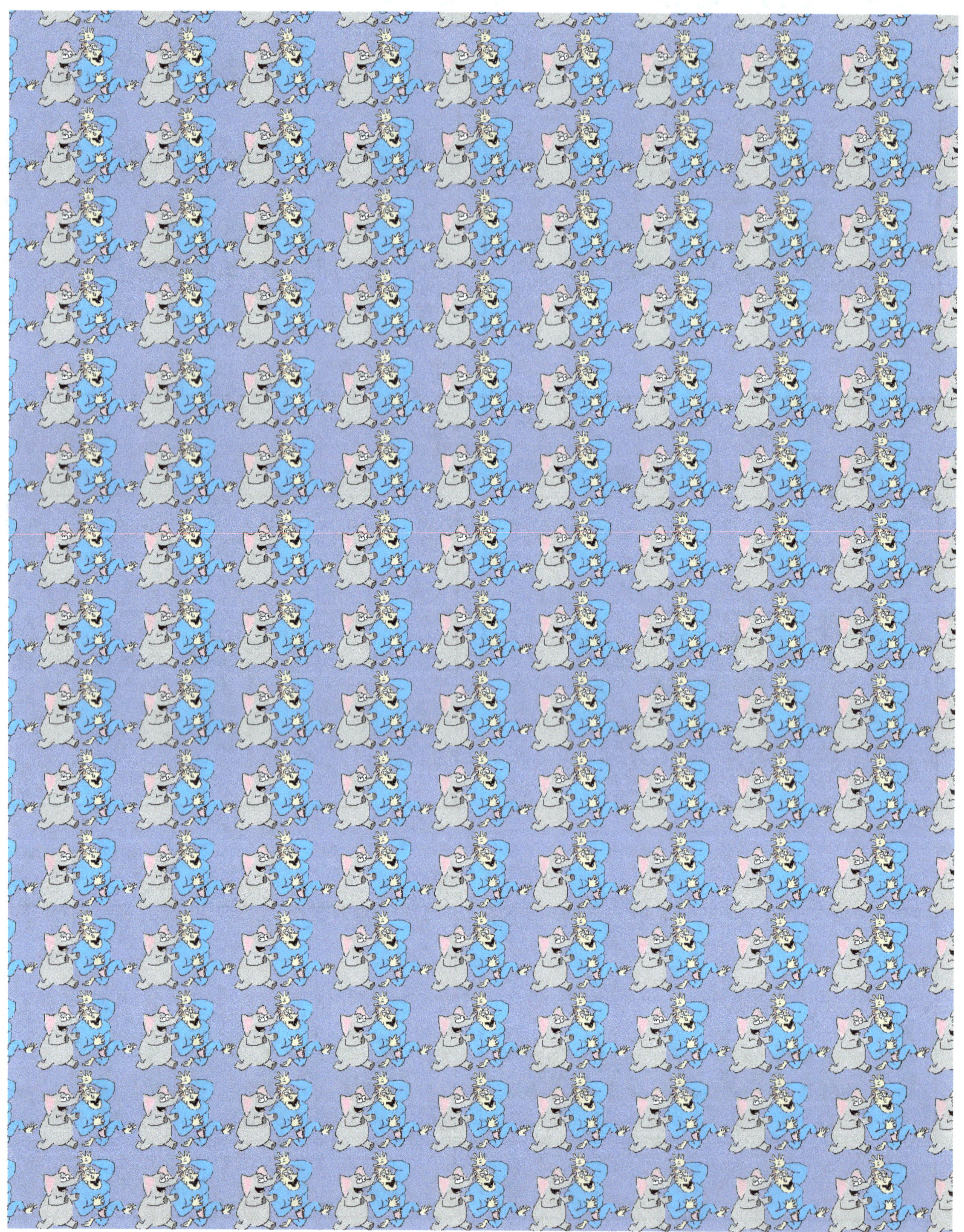

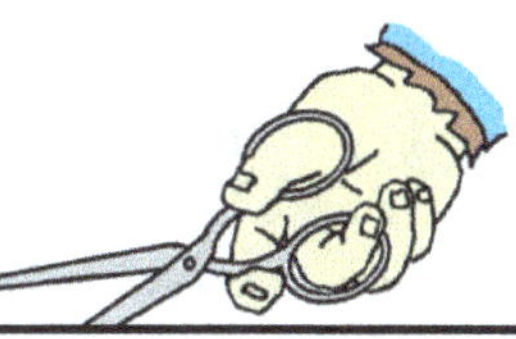

let's

what

cent

see

call

must

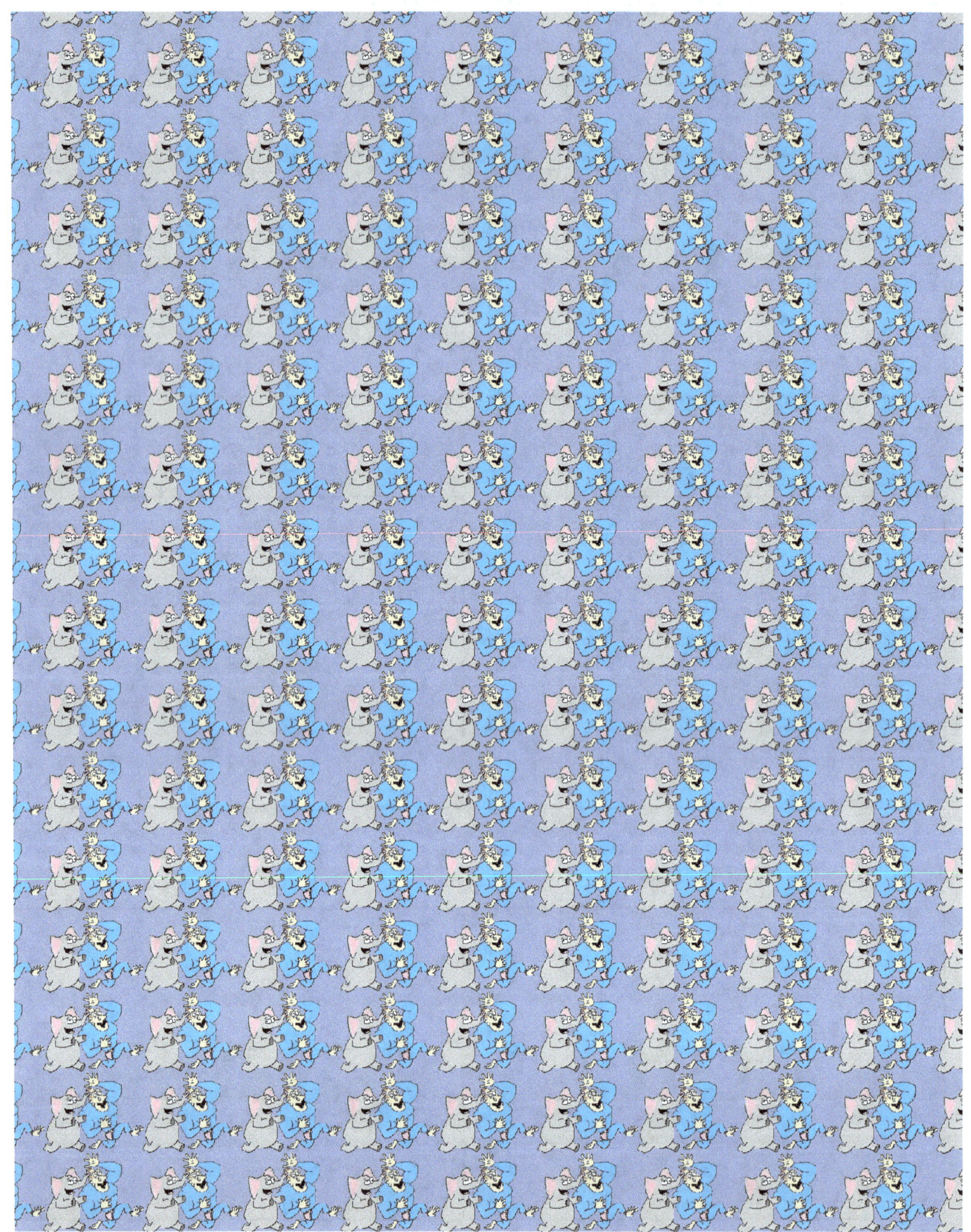

OUR SIGHT WORD FLASH CARDS!

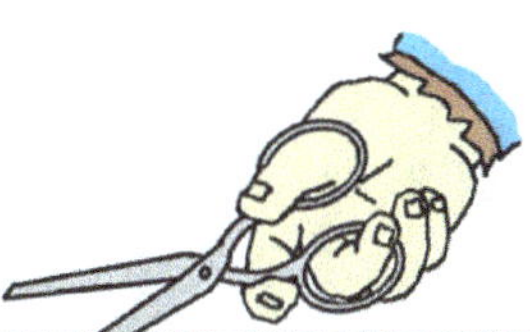

need

and

all

on

in

the

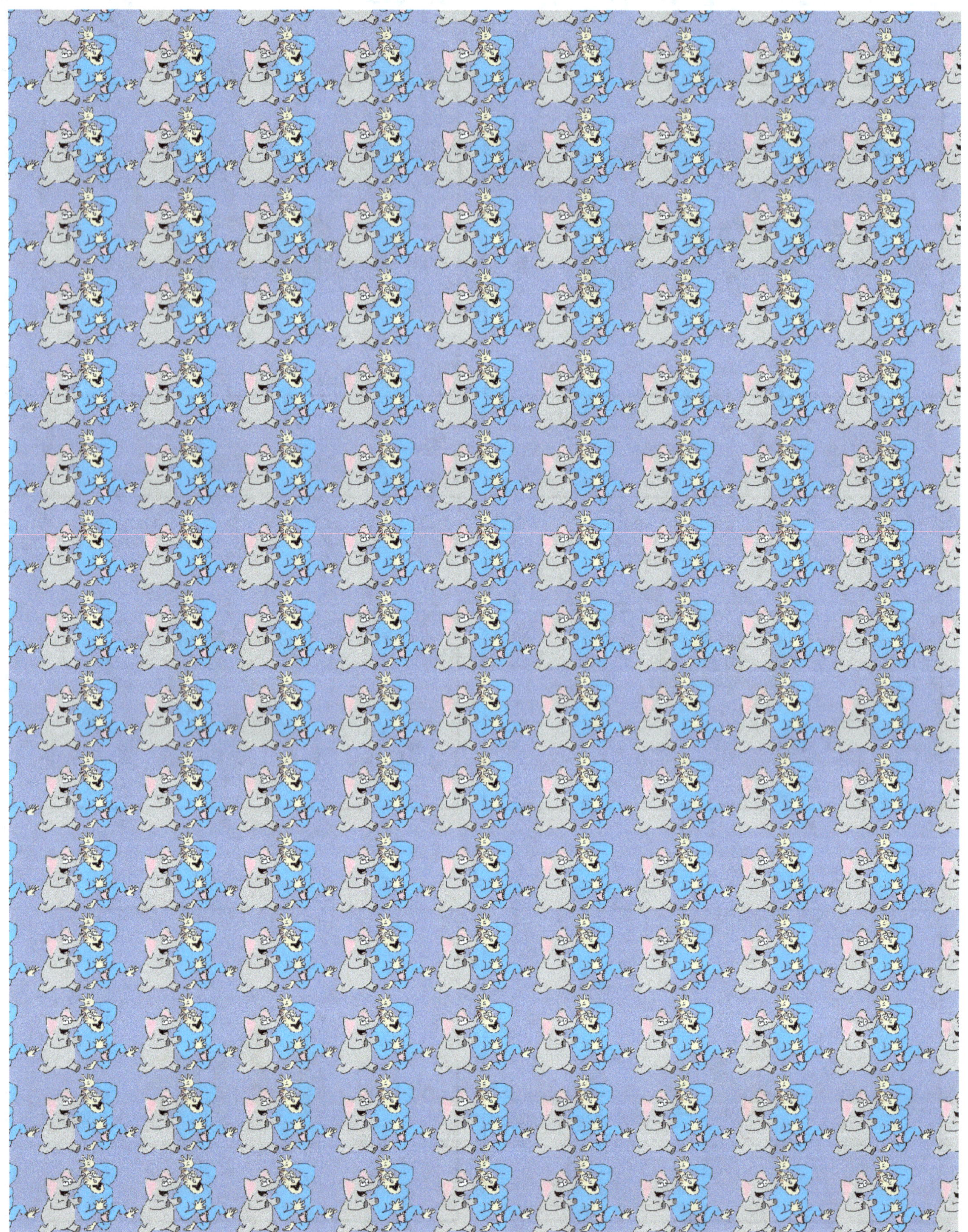

OUR SIGHT WORD FLASH CARDS!

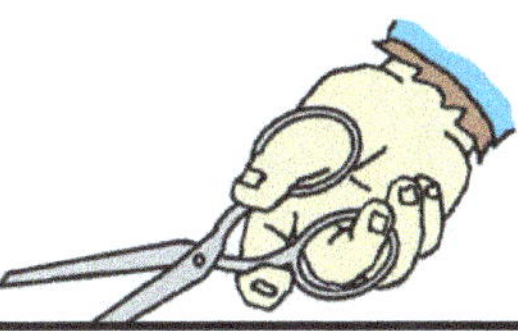

not

lift

like

get

did

you

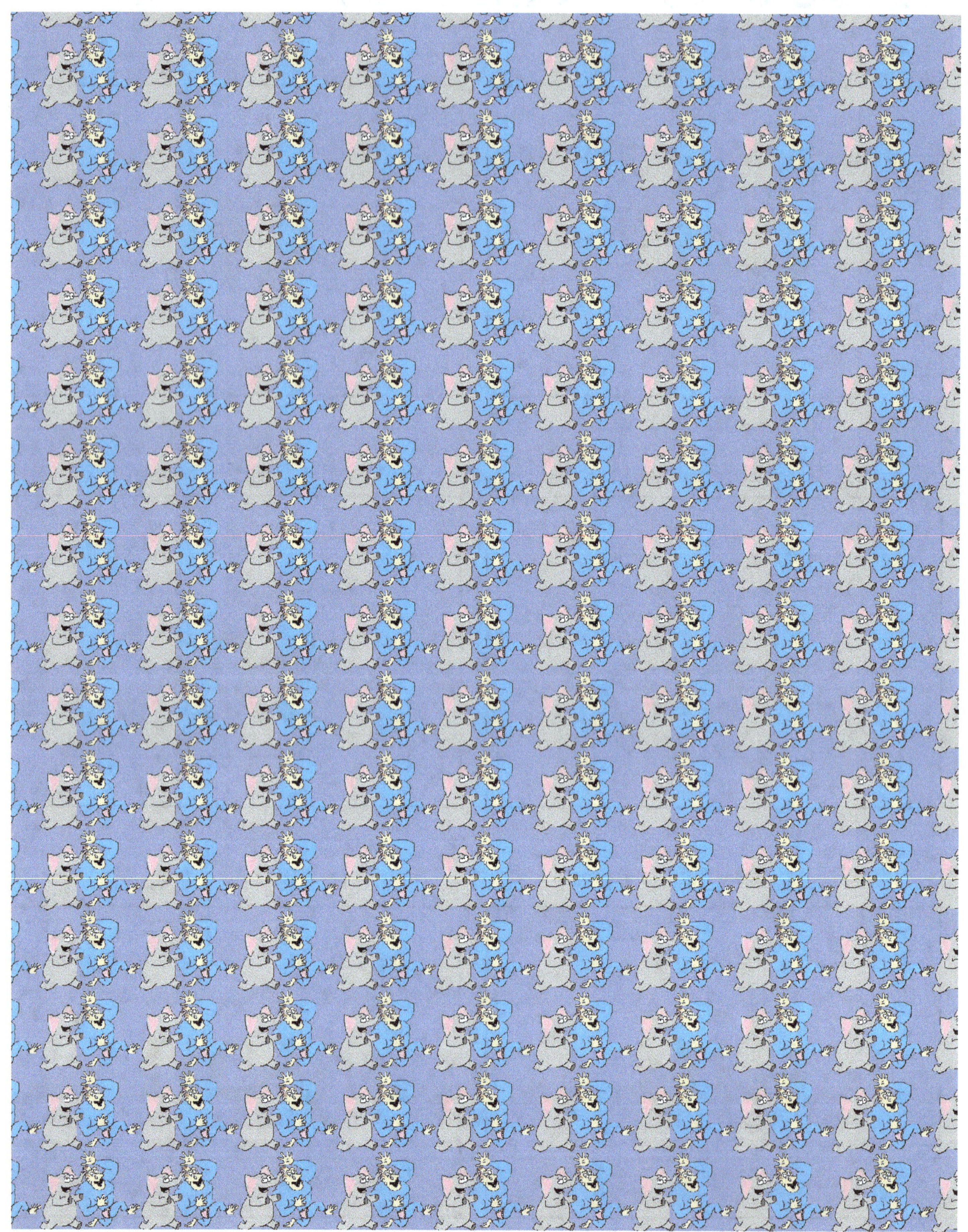

OUR SIGHT WORD FLASH CARDS!

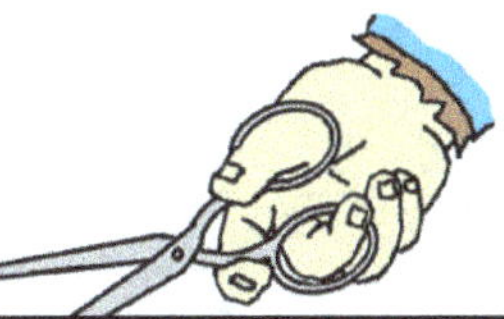

your

has

put

one

by

say

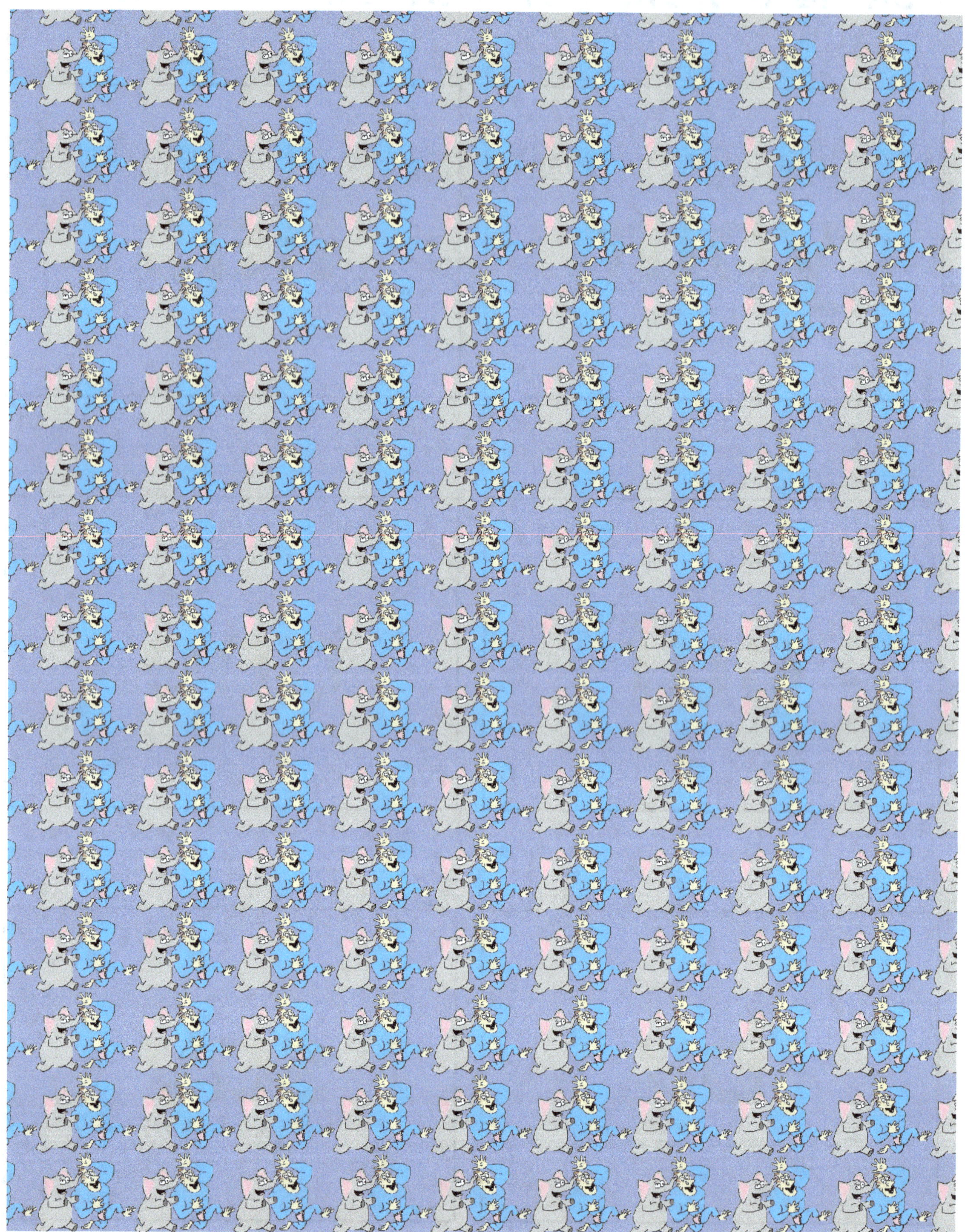

OUR SIGHT WORD FLASH CARDS!

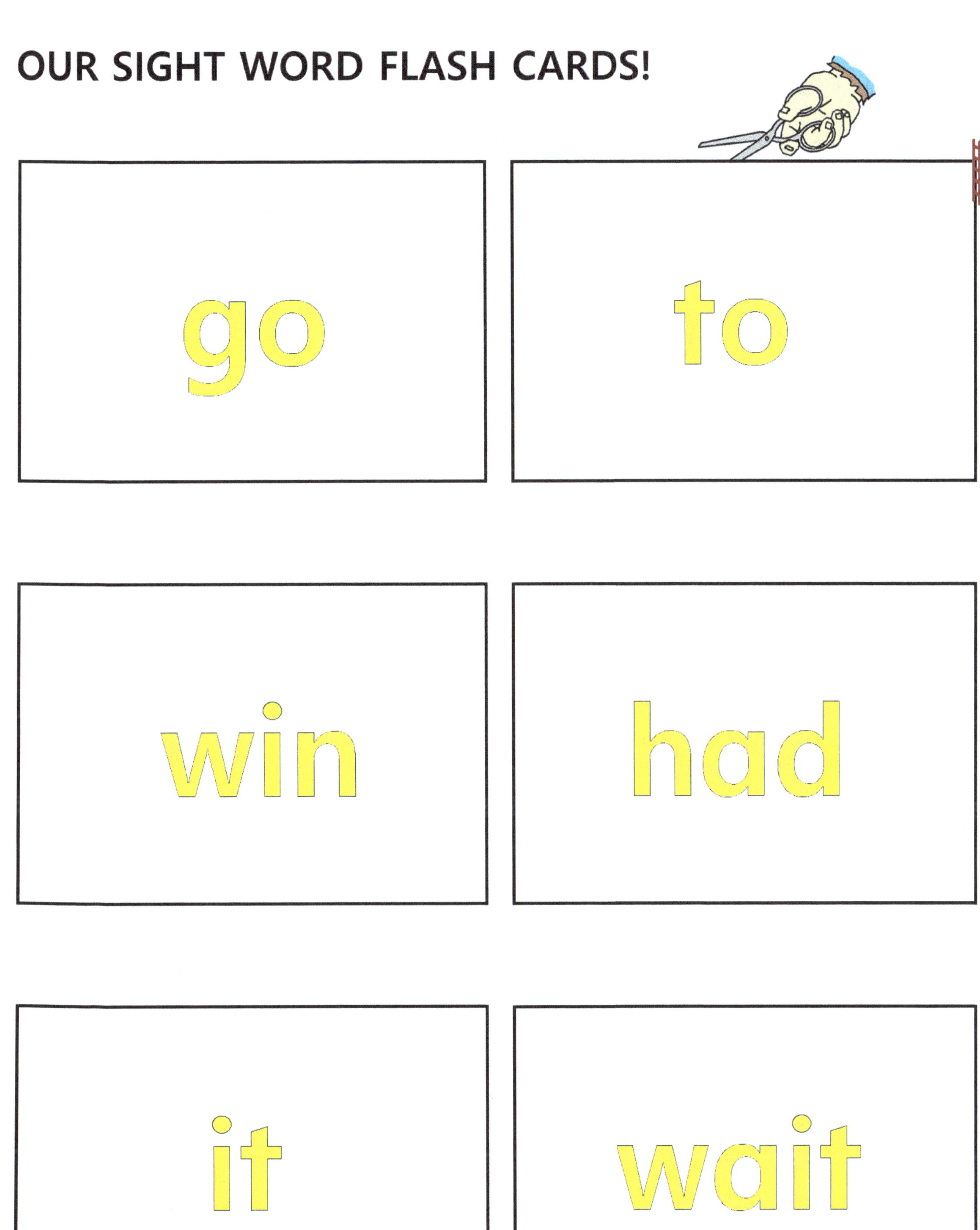

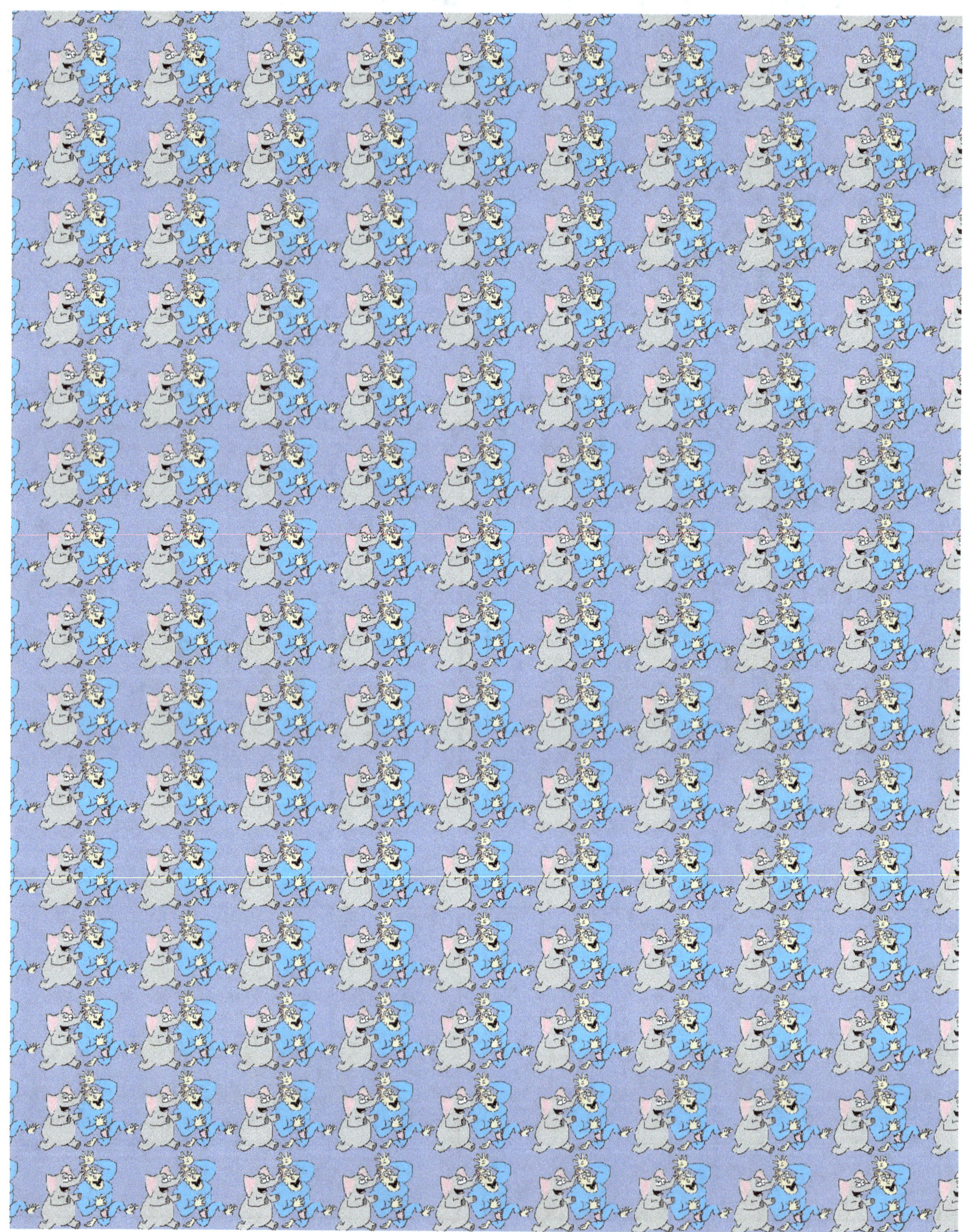

Phonics Series

Preschool:

Kindergarten:

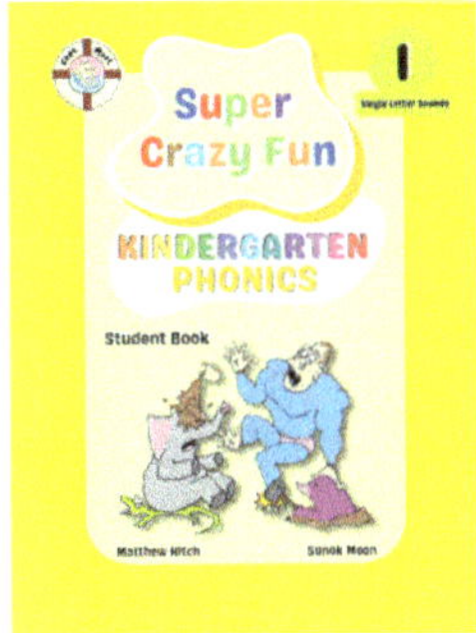

Elementary School Junior:

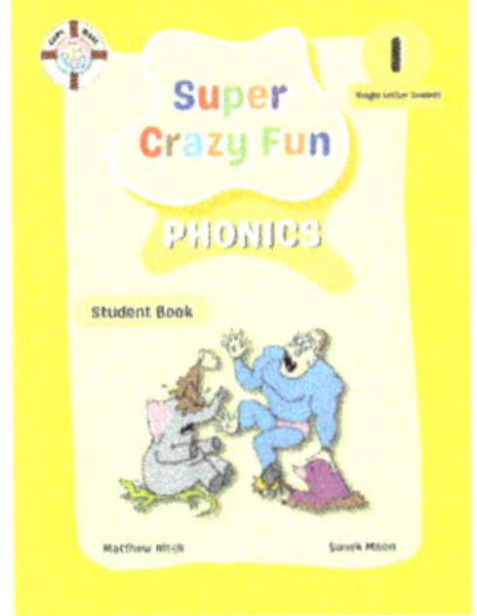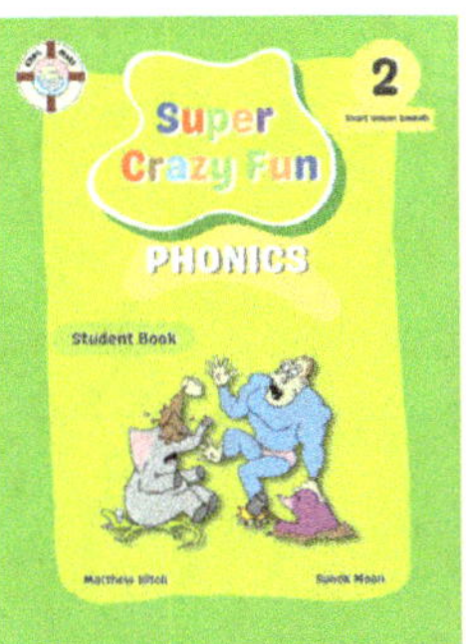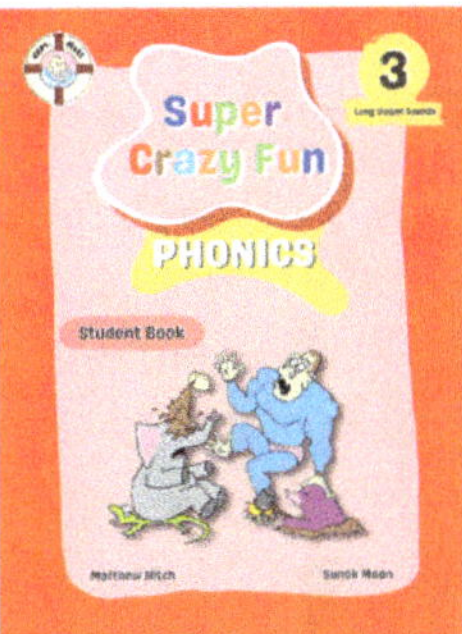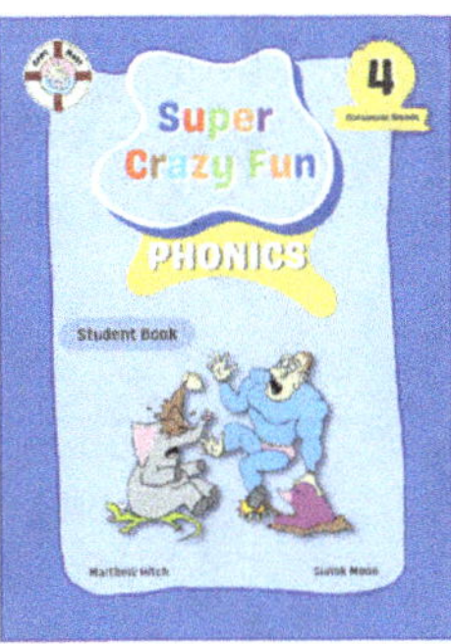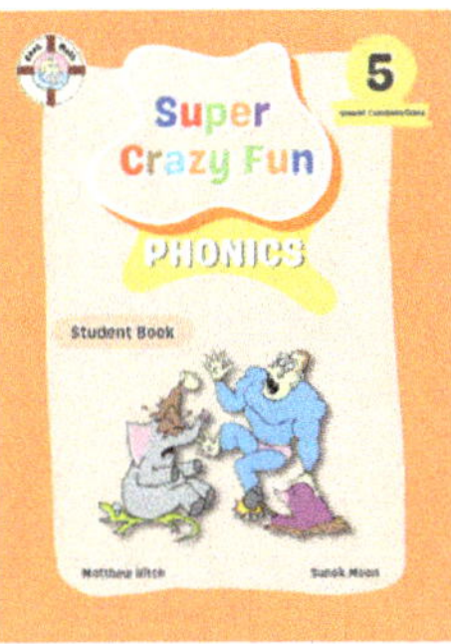

Elementary School Senior/Remedial:

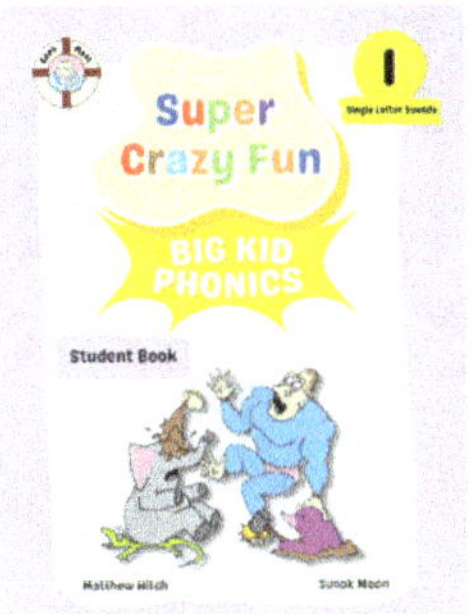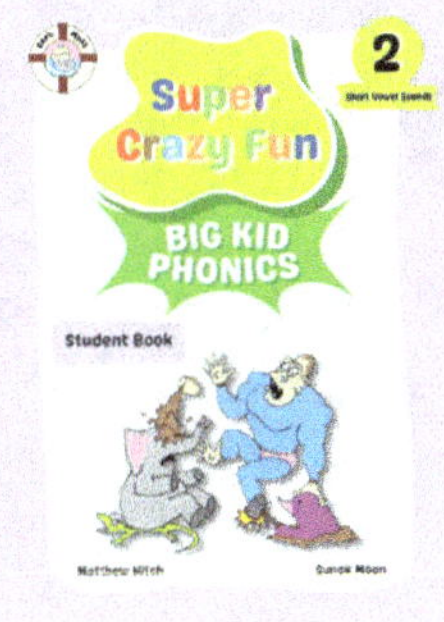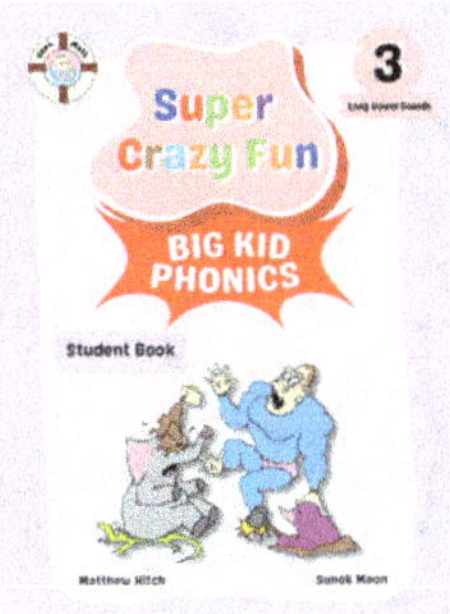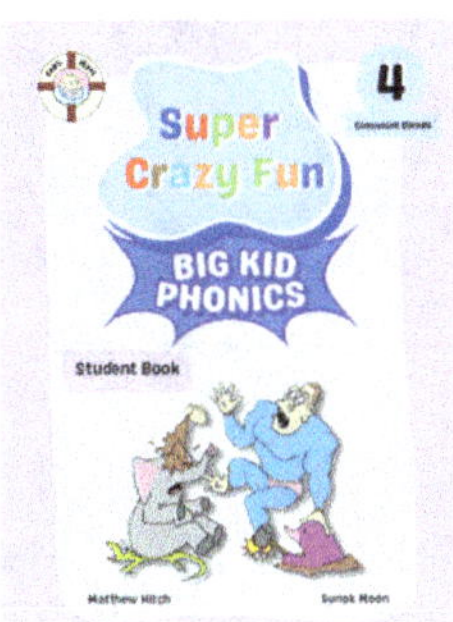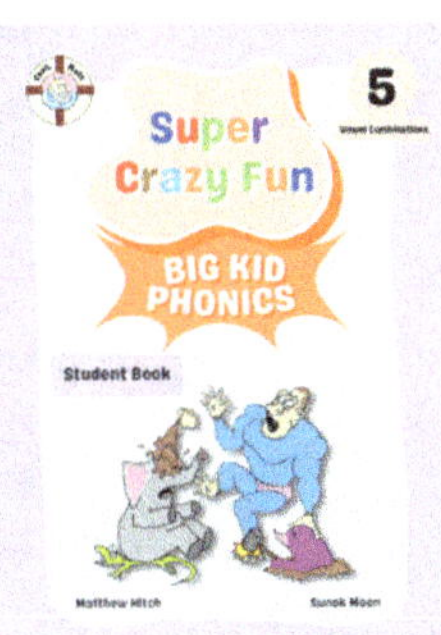

www.ingramcontent.com/pod-product-compliance
Lightning Source LLC
Chambersburg PA
CBHW060610120726
48002CB00010B/2898